T0345408

The Mothers of Manipur

THE MOTHERS OF MANIPUR

Twelve Women Who Made History

TERESA REHMAN

Introduction by
Pamela Philipose

zubaan

ZUBAAN
128 B Shahpur Jat, 1st floor
NEW DELHI 110 049
Email: contact@zubaanbooks.com
Website: www.zubaanbooks.com

First published by Zubaan Publishers Pvt. Ltd 2017

10 9 8 7 6 5 4 3 2 1

ISBN 978 93 84757 76 2

Zubaan is an independent feminist publishing house based in New Delhi with a strong academic and general list. It was set up as an imprint of India's first feminist publishing house, Kali for Women, and carries forward Kali's tradition of publishing world quality books to high editorial and production standards. *Zubaan* means tongue, voice, language, speech in Hindustani. Zubaan publishes in the areas of the humanities, social sciences, as well as in fiction, general non-fiction, and books for children and young adults under its Young Zubaan imprint.

Typeset in Minion Pro 12/16 by Jojy Philip, New Delhi 110 015
Printed and bound at Raj Press, R-3 Inderpuri, New Delhi 110 012

To my late mother Zamira Begum Rahman, nee Khan, the woman who taught me that it is the small things that make life beautiful.

Contents

Acknowledgements

The Mothers of Manipur is a story I wanted to tell the world. In the course of my reporting assignments to the trouble-torn state, I met some of these brave mothers. This book is my way of paying tribute to their courage, grit, hope and aspiration.

I have a long list of people I have to thank for making this book possible.

I thank these stellar women for sharing their lives, their joys and sorrows with me. Their words and wisdom will lead us to a better understanding of the way conflict affects the lives of women in Manipur.

This book is also my way of bringing out some of the faces behind those bomb blasts, AK 47s, curfews and protests. I thank the mothers (and other people I met), for treating me to my favourite delicacies – home-cooked rice and *iromba*. Thank you for the wisecracks, love, laughter and warm hugs. I love you, dear Imas.

This book is not a mere collection of the biographies of these 12 women. It is more. Through their stories, I try to tell the story of the resilient people of contemporary Manipur. Some of these extraordinary Manipuris ended up as characters in my book: thank you Bishwajeet Elangbam, Chanam Urmila, Akhu Chingangbam, Lin Laishram, Binalakshmi Nepram, Arambam Angamba Singh, Late Heisnam Kanhailal, Sabitri Heisnam, Irom Sharmila and members of the Manipur Network of Positive People (MNP+).

My thanks to young researcher Basanta Wareppa for helping me understand the emotions and narratives. He is meticulous and knows that documenting the lives of common people is important to comprehend how people live on the edge. Thank you, Chitra Ahanthem for accompanying me on a few occasions. Chitra is a journalist. I remember she once told me, 'I am also a Meira Paibi. But my torch is my pen.'

Thank you, Urvashi Butalia for realizing that it is important to document the lives of these women. Pooja Pande deserves thanks for running me through the drafts, and the meticulous editing. Monideepa Choudhury, who I turned to whenever I had to clarify doubts in the course of writing. Azera Rehman for reading my drafts in the midst of the din created by little Zara. Radhika MB, for the long-distance calls from New Jersey, USA to unwrap the details of the book. Guwahati-based entrepreneur, Hussina Thokchom Salam, for helping me fathom the intricate nuances of Meitei society.

Katherine Boo, I cannot thank you enough for believing in my work and writing the blurb for the book cover. And Pamela Philipose, thank you for so graciously agreeing to write an Introduction.

A host of family and friends made this book possible: my husband, Raza Rafiqul Hoque, created the cocoon where I could sit and write. Many a time, he has been both the father and mother to our daughters, Tamara and Kyra. My sister, Nazia Mehzabeen, who happily took care of my daughters whenever I was busy travelling. Anindita Das, a dear friend, cooked sumptuous meals for me whenever I needed some good food to lift my spirits. My father, Habibur Rahman, for making me what I am today. My late mother, Zamira Begum Rahman, to whom I dedicate this book on the brave mothers of Manipur.

Introduction

PAMELA PHILIPOSE

What was it about that protest which took place in 2004 that continues to resonate to this day, not just in the region where it played out but in the entire country and beyond? The images of Meira Paibis (women torch bearers of Manipur), some of them over 60 years of age, stripping outside the headquarters of the Assam Rifles at the Kangla Fort in Imphal, holds a significant place in the crowded annals of contemporary India. It is important to remember that this incident took place before the advent of platforms like Facebook and Twitter with their capacity to provide instant virality to developments far less tempestuous. Local television channel ISTV, which was present as the 12 women held their banners aloft, had their footage quickly outlawed after a brief airing, as the authorities scrambled to control the consequences of the high voltage demonstration. Yet, given its unprecedented nature, the images did go 'viral' in the immediate term and continued to be a major point of reference in the years that followed.

Before we try to answer why this was the case, it may be useful to contextualize this protest. It occurred, first of all, against the backdrop of a fissured, militarized region existing under the shadow of draconian laws. As Sanjay Barbora has pointed out, laws like the Armed Forces (Special Powers) Act, 1958 (AFSPA) and the Disturbed Areas Act may have been promulgated to address the Naga insurgency, but they ended up causing a rash of armed rebellions against the Indian state, 'If the proliferation of armed rebellion was one side of the peculiar consequences of militarization, the slow but sure erosion of civic values and sensibilities was another.'[1]

Manipur was brought under AFSPA in 1980, but far from restoring peace and a semblance of normalcy, AFSPA only exacerbated insurgent tendencies across the state, underlining the growing alienation of a large swathe of Manipuri society from the country. Among the many flashpoints that took place in Manipur in the post-AFSPA era was the Malom massacre of November 2000 that resulted in the deaths of ten innocents at the

---

[1] Barbora, Sanjay, 2016: 'Remembrance, Recounting and Resistance', in *Garrisoned Minds Women and Armed Conflict in South Asia*, New Delhi: Speaking Tiger, p. 224.

hands of the security forces. It led, in turn, to a little known woman called Irom Sharmila, then just 28 years old, embarking upon an extraordinary hunger strike for the revocation of the dreaded law. She later clarified that she undertook that fast, which was to last for 16 years, not on an emotional whim but as a 'rational being acting on my conscience'.

This hunger strike forms the second framing context. It could be argued that this unprecedented gesture undertaken by Irom Sharmila of turning her body into a weapon of resistance was a precursor to that defiant disrobing in front of the Kangla Fort four years later. If Sharmila had found succour in the firmly bonded matriarchy of the Meira Paibis who had themselves long been organizing against AFSPA, the Meira Paibis, in turn, clearly drew inspiration, while turning their bodies into sites of struggle, from Sharmila's resolute stance.

There is a third framing context that also needs to be remembered. If the silence on rape and other forms of sexualized violence perpetrated by the army had not been broken by courageous Manipuri women telling their own horrific stories of assault, it may have been impossible for the Meira Paibis to make their preposterous demand that the Indian army rape them. Thingnam Anjulika Samom argues that the public revelations of sexual assault at the hands of army personnel in the mid-1990s opened 'a Pandora's box on a subject which hitherto has been cloaked by a culture of silence' and triggered passionate demands for justice.[2] Given the prevailing social conservatism of Manipuri society, the stigma associated with rape and the ever-present fear of reprisal from the armed forces, this new willingness of women to name and shame their sexual predators constituted a major shift in their public articulation.

The trigger for the Meira Paibi action was the broken and abused body of Thangjam Manorama, with gunshot wounds on her genitals, caused by the Assam Rifles. Some of the women had visited the morgue and seen the body for themselves and, as they described its state to their sobbing colleagues, it compelled them to imagine a new language of resistance because the old ways of protest suddenly appeared shorn of meaning. It was as if their own, older bodies had to become that of Manorama's and 'offered' to her persecutors. Teresa Rehman, through her careful interviews with the '12 women who made history' that are carried in these pages, provides us with telling snatches of that interior journey, even as the late summer heat merged with the simmering tension of the moment.

What is particularly poignant in the accounts is the sense of the frailness of body pitted against the enormity of the project. These were ordinary women,

---

[2] Samom, Thingnam Anjulika, 2016: 'The Art of Defiance' in *Garrisoned Minds Women and Armed Conflict in South Asia*, New Delhi: Speaking Tiger, p. 239.

most of them vendors in Imphal's Ima Keithel (mother's market), who now had to transform themselves into an unstoppable force. Despite palpitations of the heart, fits of dizziness, insomnia, failing eyesight, the planning for that action had to be meticulous: inner garments had to be removed leaving only the *enaphi* and *phanek* (the upper and lower garment) to make the act of stripping swifter, jewellery needed to be tied in little bundles and kept in safe custody and, above all, utmost secrecy had to be maintained with not even close family members being informed in order to ensure that the authorities didn't get wind of their plans.

The element of surprise was one of the major reasons for the success of the protest and its subsequent transition into legend. The police and armed forces in the state had witnessed all kinds of protests, from mass rallies and torchlit marches to hunger strikes and black flag demonstrations, and knew well enough how to respond to them. But this particular incident went beyond anything laid down in SOP manuals.

In their interviews with Teresa Rehman, each of the mothers remembered vividly the moment of confrontation as they shook the gates of Kangla, both literally and metaphorically. Perhaps the most detailed account emerged from Ima Nganbi, best known for having shouted in English, 'Indian army rape us. Take our flesh.' She herself carried two banners with this message under her armpit, which were then unfurled before the busy morning crowds. What is significant about her narration are the details she provided on the conversation the women had with those guarding the gate, and the manner in which they drew on their social authority as older women to confront them. They even referred to the Manipuri convention which bestows power on their phanek, a garment that strange men cannot touch without being cursed for life. The observations of Deepti Priya Mehrotra are moot in this context, 'Deliberately exposing their bodies, the women simultaneously asserted their right to their own bodies. Rejecting the masculinist definition of women's bodies as attractive or unattractive, available or unavailable, they moved into an entirely different paradigm.'[3] That their action transcended the immediate moments of its occurrence, testified to its success in transferring the shame attached to the act of rape from assaulted women like Manorama, to the army. By perpetrating and condoning such acts through its deliberate silences and active counter propaganda, the institution of the army had been rendered a dishonourable one.

The symbolism of stripping that was in focus here was not just of clothes but of human flesh. The slogans shouted at the sexual predator in uniform included words like

---

[3] Mehrotra, Deepti Priya, 2010: 'Restoring Order in Manipur' in Preeti Gill (ed.) *The Peripheral Centre: Voices from India's Northeast*, New Delhi: Zubaan, p. 224.

'flesh us', 'eat our flesh'. The anger that was driving these women also made them want to consume the uniformed sentinels that stood before them. As Ima Ibetombi put it in her interview, 'If the police came forward we would have torn their pants and shirts. We were like Goddess Kali – ready to devour.' It was this visceral aspect that added a strongly emotional dimension to their actions and captured the popular imagination. Yet, somewhere deep inside, there was also a sense of violation. Ima Mema believed that by exposing herself to the world she had lost all her privacy and dignity, 'It was almost like raping oneself.'

Two other factors added to the memorialization of these moments that recalled the familiar Milan Kundera quotation, 'The struggle of man against power is the struggle of memory against forgetting.' Over time the Meira Paibis turned into their own historians, keeping the Kangla Fort action alive through the constant telling and re-telling of their stories. State censorship is flat-footed and cannot keep up with the swiftness and pervasiveness of personal accounts and the depth of that all-encompassing commons which is popular memory. Both the army and the Manipur state government took all manner of measures to put a lid on the telling of these tales. They imposed curfews, threatened intimidation and cracked down on the media, but their efforts only seemed to channel more wind into the sails of the women's narratives.

The Meira Paibis themselves were natural raconteurs, carefully piecing together the mosaic of that morning, every single detail meticulously put in place. They also instinctively understood the importance of media coverage, as Ima Jibanmala indicated, 'When newspapers flashed our photo, I felt violated. But I felt it was also important to highlight our cause in the media.'

Even as time aged their bodies – one among them died in 2013 – they lost no opportunity to pass on the whole account to emerging generations, building for themselves bridges of empathy to friend and stranger alike. Their accounts indicate a sophisticated sense of honing in on what is important. There is, for instance, in the interview that Teresa Rehman did with Ima Jamini, this explanation offered for the rare bonding that existed between the Meira Paibis which was ultimately what made the Kangla Fort protest possible: 'Once we are out of the house and are with women, we don't care about our family and mundane affairs. Ours is a community in itself. We don't care what husbands, sons or our daughters-in-law will think. We feel empowered to take our own decisions.'

The other factor that has helped to memorialize the 'naked protest' was the fact that it had inspired and been the subject of innumerable creative enactments and reenactments. Mahasweta Devi's well-known play 'Draupadi', which dealt with army atrocities against women in the country's Naxalite areas, became almost a template for the Kangla Fort protest and may have even inspired it in an indirect way. This book cites the version of the play staged in Imphal earlier which had been directed by the late Kanhailal and featured his wife Sabitri Heisnam as the protagonist. This work took on new meaning after the 'naked protest'. Additions were made and the telling sentence 'Indian army rape us' now rang out on the stage. Similarly, videos and still images of the protest, now widely available on the internet, have been used by documentalists of all kinds, from journalists to film makers. Amar Kanwar's 'Lightning Testimonies', to cite one instance, used the protest footage alongside theatrical enactments.

The protest brought national and international attention to hitherto faceless women, but once the intense solidarities of the moment melted away, they also had to cope with the significant social and emotional costs. In at least one case it led to serious family discord, as Teresa Rehman reveals. Ima Sarojini now stays away from her family and comes in occasionally to visit her daughter and granddaughter. Her husband is full of resentment over his wife's independence, wondering aloud whether she will even be there when he dies. Similarly, when Thingam Anjulika Samom visited some of the Meira Paibis in 2013, she found many suffering from various health conditions and she quoted the head of the Department of Clinical Psychology at the Regional Institute of Medical Sciences in Imphal as saying, 'Exposing their naked bodies in front of the Kangla Fort was the culmination of a phase of mental disquiet.'[4] Ima Ibemhal recalled having fainted after the protest and Ima Mema still cannot shake off the fear that now suffuses her life. Every time her granddaughter goes out alone, she is gripped by an inexplicable anxiety. It is a fear that Ima Momon, whose son writes songs that could be deemed as subversive by the authorities, is very familiar with because it marks every hour of her day. 'I fear for his life. I am anxious all the time,' she said.

The awareness that this protest – for which they had put aside their notions of honour – has not led to any systemic change in Manipur, is a huge disappointment for these women, and diminishes in their mind the few positive outcomes of their action. The hope of any real justice being delivered over the Manorama killing quickly proved to be an illusion, with the Assam Rifles refusing point blank to cooperate in the inquiry. Those who perpetrated the assault were not even identified, much less brought to book. The Rs 10 lakh that the family received through a Supreme Court order a full decade later can be little consolation when her killers continue to roam free.

The army vacated Kangla Fort and AFSPA was withdrawn from seven assembly constituencies within

---

[4] Samom, Anjulika Thingnam, 2013: 'Ill & Frail, and Yet Going Strong', *Deccan Herald/WFS*.

the Imphal municipal area, these were the minor concessions made to assuage the sentiments of the protestors. But they know only too well that the writ of that law continues to run. Every day brings its share of army intrusions into homes. The picking up of innocents, encounter deaths and daily patrolling remain very much a part of Manipur's everyday reality. Two government-appointed committees, the Justice Jeevan Reddy Committee and the Justice Verma Committee, submitted their findings in 2005 and 2013 respectively. The first recommended the repealing of the act; the second suggested that there should be a review of its continuance and noted that 'systematic or isolated sexual violence, in the process of Internal Security duties, is being legitimised by the Armed Forces (Special Powers) Act.' In both instances, pressure from the army ensured that the draconian law remained on the statute books and without any changes.

With all its heroic strengths, a community-focused organization like the Meira Paibis has inevitably had to wrestle with real dilemmas that have, in turn, exposed the women's own inadequacies of judgment and response. Because their activism against rape arose largely out of their sense of solidarity with their own community, the Meiteis, and not from a feminist understanding of the gendered nature of the crime, they were often silent when it was the valley-based underground groups, rather than the army, that were being accused of such violence. Stances driven by such self-interest severely undermined their claim that they represented all the women of Manipur.

In the Irom Sharmila case too, their unilinear worldview was found completely out of sync with reality. Having come to regard Irom Sharmila as an icon of Manipur's struggle, a being to be revered almost like a goddess, they were bitterly opposed to her decision to give up her hunger strike after over a decade and a half. So caught up were they in this myth of their own making that they could not understand Sharmila when she said she wanted to be a 'revolutionary, not a martyr', that she wanted to live and struggle against AFSPA in a manner different from what they had envisaged for her.

Both these instances appear to indicate that by the second decade of the 21st century, the Meira Paibis had found themselves in a time warp. They had now been in public activism for over three decades but the changing world demanded a re-imagining of their role as social activists. A lack of intellectual resources and physical stamina made such a proposition impossible. This, of course, is a great pity because the present times of vicious ethnic, communal and gender-centric violence in the country, including in a state like Manipur, demand wider participation of women. As political science academics have argued, 'It is the institutionalization of a more humane and feminized worldview that will most effectively lead to the kind of conflict resolution most compatible with the wider agenda of a truly transformative politics.'[5]

Yet, it also needs to be emphasized that recognizing their limitations does not in the least take away from the inherent heroism and capacity for social action of the Meira Paibis. The conversations in this book make these women born to bear torches come alive in intimate ways.

---

[5] Chenoy, Anuradha M. and Achin Vanaik, 2001: 'Promoting Peace, Security and Conflict Resolution: Gender Balance in Decision making', in Inger Skjelsbaek and Dan Smith: *Gender, Peace & Conflict*, New Delih: Sage Publications, p. 137.

Thangjam Manorama (1970–2004) was picked up from her home by troops of the 17th Assam Rifles on 10 July 2004, on charges of being associated with a banned militant outfit, the People's Liberation Army (PLA) of Manipur, India.

The next morning, her bullet-ridden corpse with bruise marks, allegedly of sexual assault, was found in a field. The Assam Rifles claimed that she had been shot while trying to escape.

There were widespread protests in reaction to this incident, including the unprecedented nude protest by elderly women on 15 July 2004, in front of the Assam Rifles headquarters at Kangla Fort in Imphal. A commission of inquiry was set up under retired judge C. Upendra Singh by the Manipur government, which submitted its report in November 2004.

In 2005, the Jeevan Reddy Committee, set up to review the Armed Forces (Special Powers) Act, 1958 (AFSPA) recommended that AFSPA should be repealed. In 2013 the Justice Verma Committee, set up to suggest amendments to laws relating to crimes against women, recommended a review of the continuance of AFSPA in the context of providing legal protection to women in conflict areas.

Meanwhile, the Supreme Court in December 2014 directed the government to pay Rs 1,000,000 as interim compensation to the mother of Thangjam Manorama. This book tells the story of how and why the twelve women who took part in the nude protest came together, and what happened to their lives afterwards. In doing so, it seeks out the stories of many others, the women of Manipur, who keep the flame alive.

Preface

An Oath is Taken

14 July 2004, 7 am

The office of Macha Leima, a women's organization, in Palace Compound, Imphal, the capital city of Manipur.

There is a stillness in the early morning air. The sun's rays are intense, they signal that the day will be hot and oppressive. Power cuts are common in this small northeastern Indian city, and this angers people; today this anger is further fuelled by the tension that has been simmering ever since 32-year-old Thangjam Manorama was found on 11 July, brutally raped and killed.

The killing triggered an outpouring of rage; there were huge rallies and demonstrations, and several closed-door meetings. The meeting in the office of Macha Leima is, however a different one, out of the ordinary. A group of women has already assembled in the rather spartan room that is located in a corner of the L-shaped building which also houses a school for girls. The room has a table, a few chairs and a couple of framed black and white photographs on the walls that testify to the quiet passage of glory. None of the women present has any inkling that their discussions today will lead them to a resolve that will carve their names in the annals of history. They are elderly women, grandmothers and mothers, united in the pain of helplessly watching their daughters endure abuse and violation. In the room, their grief is palpable; so is their dread of what the future holds.

Formally known as Manipuri Chanura Leishem Marup, Macha Leima was set up in 1969 for the socio-economic 'uplift' of women. Over the years, this room has been witness to many closed-door meetings and scores of workshops and training programmes on issues such as micro-finance, the Right to Information, child rights and more. No meeting, though, has been as filled with despair as this one. None had fear lurking in the shadows.

There is an initial exchange of pleasantries. One woman curses the power cuts. Two others who have brought *humais* or handmade fans, pass them around. For a while, all one hears is the brisk movement of the fans, taking the edge off the stifling heat inside the room. Someone brings up the death of Manorama and, as if on cue, all eyes moisten. She reconstructs the shocking details of the rape, the torture and finally, the killing by the security forces. She tells them how Manorama's body was found mutilated – full of cuts, a cloth inserted inside her vagina. 'They even shot at her vagina to destroy all evidence of rape,' she says in anguish.

It is not the first time that something so monstrous has occurred. Such happenings have become routine in the state, just as protests have. An indefinite curfew has been on in Imphal and its surrounding areas since 11 July. But, defying the authorities, the people continue to stage sit-ins, protests and mass rallies. Apunba Lup, an umbrella group of civil society organizations, has been holding meetings and chalking out strategies. Nevertheless, a sense of despondency and a pall of gloom have descended on this beautiful land.

At the Macha Leima office, Manorama's death has forced the women to take a closer look at their own plight, and the situation in the state. They feel compelled to take a radical decision: they want to do something that will make a difference, something strong which reflects their anger. There is an animated exchange of stories as they revisit the past and the history of Manipuri women, fearless, undaunted, especially during the Nupi Lans of 1904 and 1939, wars waged by women against mass exploitation and famine during British imperialism. The 1904 Nupi Lan set off after the men of Imphal were ordered to carry wood and bamboo from Kabow Valley in Burma and reconstruct the fire-ravaged residence of Major Maxwell, the British Political Agent in Manipur. The women responded by coming out in large numbers on the streets. There was bloodshed, but the uprising successfully managed to rescind the Agent's order. The 1939 Nupi Lan was triggered by the policy of exporting rice at a time when Manipur was on the verge of a famine. For several months, the women struggled unarmed against military and police force before the movement ended with the outbreak of World War I.

The buzz in the room grows louder as more and more opinions are voiced. One thing leads to another and a number of ideas are laid on the table: someone suggests taking out a silent protest with black bands across the mouth, there's an idea for a bicycle rally with slogans shouted all over Imphal, a third idea is for an indefinite hunger strike. But all of them seem hackneyed and do not hold the imagination of the women. Suddenly, one woman pitches a radical idea: she remembers seeing a photograph of a nude male protester in a magazine once and she wonders if they can do something similar. A nude protest which, of course, would not be easy at all.

The women look at each other. All of them seem uncomfortable at the thought. It is a challenge. However, things have come to such a pass that they require action that shocks. The usual demonstrations and peaceful agitations demanding punishment have so far been ineffectual in putting an end to the excesses of the security personnel. An absolute revocation of the draconian Armed Forces (Special Powers) Act, (AFSPA)

1958, in force to curb the activities of 20-odd militant outfits operating in the state, is the need of the hour.

AFSPA gives the armed forces wide powers to shoot, arrest and search – all in the name of 'aiding civil power'. The army can shoot to kill, it can enter and search without a warrant and it can destroy property. Section 4 of the Act grants unrestricted power to the security forces to carry out their operations in a 'disturbed area'. In fact, even a non-commissioned officer has been granted the right to shoot to kill on mere suspicion and in order to 'maintain the public order'. Time and again there have been protests demanding a repeal of the Act. A young Manipuri woman, Irom Sharmila, has also been fasting since 2 November 2000 demanding the Act's withdrawal from the state. Thirty-three-year-old Sharmila is under judicial detention and continues to be nose-fed forcibly at the Jawaharlal Nehru Hospital in Imphal for refusing to end her 'fast unto death'. [Sharmila has since ended her fast, having decided to continue her battle by fighting for political power.]

There is a moment of silence. The sound of collective and somewhat nervous heartbeats seems to fill the stuffy room. The women of Macha Leima finally come to the decision that they are all Manorama's mothers, and that they will collectively take the oath to strip naked, in full public glare, in front of the gates of the Assam Rifles headquarters at Kangla Fort in the heart of Imphal. The choice of venue is crucial too – Kangla Fort is emblematic of Manipur's glorious past. Until 1891, it was the ancient capital of the Meitei rulers of Manipur. Now, it is the headquarters of the country's oldest paramilitary force, the Assam Rifles – which is in charge of counter-insurgency operations in the state. A force that was raised in 1835, the Assam Rifles is administered by the Union Home Ministry and is primarily responsible for guarding the Indo-Myanmar border. It is stationed in Northeast India, with its apex control headquarters in Shillong, Meghalaya. Manorama, it is believed, was picked up by Assam Rifles personnel and brought to Kangla Fort for interrogation.

The room resonates with the strength of the oath. One of the women speaks up after the oath is taken and adds to the vow. The decision to strip naked in public should also be a personal choice, she says, only those women who are at ease with the idea should volunteer, there can be no second thoughts. Most importantly, only older women with wrinkled and sagging skin should participate. The purpose of the protest is not to titillate, but to provoke action that upholds the dignity of Manipuri women.

The modus operandi is discussed. Since the Kangla Fort gate is located near a busy traffic roundabout in the heart of Imphal, it is decided that the women will stand at different corners in separate groups. The signal to start the protest will be a gentle removal of the enaphi, a garment that is wrapped like a shawl. Action is fixed for 10 am on 15 July, an ideal time since the streets are filled with office-goers and business people, as well as those setting up small stalls. The protest will last for 30 minutes and the women will go by the large clock on the wall of the nearby Gandhi Memorial Hall.

It is decided that the women will shout slogans and start stripping. Once the protest begins, two groups will hold two banners and face security personnel at the gates of the Kangla Fort and gradually, as the crowd gathers, they will face the public. In case the security personnel try to assault them, they will all huddle together and lie down on the ground. The decision will be kept a closely-guarded secret because any leak could spell disaster. If the authorities learn about the planned protest, they will try to stop them.

The women agree that nobody will discuss this with anyone, not even their husbands or other family members. A deep and intense sense of bonding prompts them to join hands and break into a silent prayer.

It is resolved that the slogans on the two banners used during the protest will be simple. 'Indian Army Rape Us' and 'Take Our Flesh'. But the banner has to be painted overnight and by someone who can be trusted. One of them calls in a painter she knows well. He is taken into a room, the details are explained to him and he is made to swear that he will not reveal the plan to anyone. He is not given details of where and when though, all he's told is that there will be a protest, yet another protest. He is given money to buy white sheets and red paint and the instruction is categorical: be at the Macha Leima office before dawn.

The meeting that began at 7 am in the morning goes on until 3 pm. The media are not informed, except ISTV, the local television channel. They are also only told that a protest is planned, and that it will take place near Kangla Fort at 10 am on 15 July. There is no hint about the nature of the protest.

Finally, the women decide it's time to go home, concentrate on the protest and pray to the Almighty to give them the strength to execute their decision. The action they have chosen is an extraordinary one, never done before. The action they're going to take, they feel, will reflect their anger and will help their struggle.

15 July 2004, 7 am

The women start gathering at the Macha Leima office early in the morning. The painter who came in with the two banners is asked to leave immediately. The banners are folded and dedicated to God Phakhangba (believed to be the first king of Manipur).

Today, the room wears a grim look. The women are bleary-eyed and filled with anxiety. Most of them have not slept the previous night, caught in the excitement of making an impactful protest, the fear of the consequences of their action and the fear, ingrained in them, of exposing their bodies.

Now, the moment is upon them: they are at the cusp of redefining dissent not only in Manipur, but also in the entire world. They are convinced that their decision has been ordained by God. They remove their jewellery and wrap it in a piece of cloth. Then they remove their inner garments and huddle together in a circle, promising to tell the world about the situation in Manipur. As the time to leave for the Kangla Fort draws near, they start crying and embracing each other.

Earlier, only ten women had decided to participate in the protest, but at the last moment, two others – Gyaneswari and Ibetombi – spontaneously decided to join in. The women now disperse and make their way to the Fort. Once there, they station themselves in the south, north and west corners of the traffic island. Women volunteers join them and are asked to stand and collect their clothes.

Sharp at 10 am, the women launch their protest. Sarojini is the first to strip. Nganbi, the only woman who speaks English shouts, 'We are all Manorama's mothers. Come and rape us.' The others join in, crying and shouting in their mother tongue. The volunteers stand, shell-shocked, and somehow manage to collect the protesters' clothes and help them hold the banner.

The security men at the gate are appalled and step back. The women continue to shout as if in a trance and the crowds swell to witness a sight that is as nightmarish as it is astounding.

It is then that the commanding officer of Assam Rifles comes out. He looks at the women, folds his hands in a Namaste, bows and leaves. The police and a fleet of ambulances also arrive. A few of the protestors have fainted and are taken to a hospital. The volunteers help the others put on their clothes and then return to the Macha Leima office. Since there is a fear that the police might arrest them, they disperse one by one. However, nobody is arrested until much later. Also, charges are dropped within three months and they are released.

The extraordinary protest by the 12 mothers of Manipur left the entire state machinery in confusion. As a precautionary measure, the Manipur government imposed indefinite curfew in the Imphal East and West districts from 11 am on 15 July. The Deputy Commissioner of Imphal West issued orders under Section 19 of The Cable Television Network Regulation Act, 1995, prohibiting the transmission of any programme, including news, by the local media.

In the meantime, Manorama's lifeless body lies in the Regional Institute of Medical Sciences morgue for 13 days since her family refuses to claim it unless they get justice. Finally, on 24 July 2004, the body is declared 'unclaimed' and, under strict security, cremated by the government at the Minuthong Hatta public crematorium. On 30 July, a mass rally is organized by Apunba Lup and clashes break out between the police and protesters in many parts of Imphal.

15 July 2004 will forever remain imprinted in every Manipuri's heart. The iconic protest will continue to trigger debate and stand out in collective memory. It will always speak of the turmoil of people trapped in a world chock-full of violence. It will always reflect the larger story of Manipur – a land torn asunder by conflict and brutality, but constantly exerting the might of its cultural traditions and humane spirit, to triumph.

1

Ima Mutum Ibemhal, aka Ima Ibemhal: The Wise Shopkeeper

Khwairamband Bazaar in Imphal is a vibrant marketplace. It is also very soulful and I have invariably felt a sense of catharsis on all my visits here. I have also felt a sense of hope – somehow that there is hope beyond the conflict. Run entirely by women and fondly called the Ima Market or Ima Keithel Ima (meaning mother), it occupies a unique position, not only in the history of Manipur, but also in the hearts of its people.

Today, as I sit chatting with a group of vegetable vendors, I can sniff the mouthwatering aroma of fried savouries floating in the air. Nearby, in a tiny eatery popularly called *hoten*, I see a woman frying *boras*. She is also selling tea and *singju*, *kaanghou* and *paaknam*, and I feel tempted to try them. But, just as I am about to step across, the regular *chaiwalla* strolls over with his kettle and stacked plastic cups.

Sarita Devi, the dewy-eyed steel utensils vendor I had made friends with earlier, yells out, 'One cup here.'

I give up the idea of munching on *boras* and settle back to sip on raw tea laced with jaggery. I watch, amused, as Sarita brags loudly, pointing towards me, 'She is a famous journalist from Delhi.' (I was working for the *Tehelka* news magazine at the time.)

'Guwahati,' I correct her, 'although I travel to Delhi quite often.'

A woman lets out a sigh and asks, 'Delhi? How far is Delhi?'

Before I can answer, Sarita exclaims, 'I have been to Delhi. I know how to get there.'

The revelation causes a buzz of conversation and Sarita gets busy explaining. 'Delhi is far and took me quite long to reach. First was a long bus journey, more than 18 hours, to reach Guwahati in Assam. The roads were dreadful, which is why I have ended up with a backache. Then, I was stranded for nearly 10 hours at the Guwahati railway station because the North East Express to Delhi was running late. I was feeling sick. I could not eat anything. I sat in the crowded second class waiting room at the station, not venturing out even for a minute because I feared someone would steal my luggage. I was also scared since I was travelling alone.

'When the arrival of the North East Express was announced, I rushed out with the other passengers and clambered on to the train. I also managed to find my seat. It was my first rail journey and I was excited. But it took more than 48 hours to reach Delhi! The way to Delhi is an arduous one,' she concludes empathetically.

One of the women pitches in, 'What if a bridge is built from Imphal to Delhi?'

This seems to stir their collective imagination and ideas pour forth. There is animated discussion and much laughter on how a bridge from Imphal to Delhi would look – a long one over mountains, valleys, rivers and dales. The mirth is so infectious that one of the women nearly topples over with laughter from the platform where she sits perched with her basket of vegetables.

❧

Ima Market is eulogized by the national and international media as one of the finest examples of women's empowerment. But, as I cast my eyes around this famous marketplace, I can clearly recall a surprising observation made during a conversation by Rajesh Hijam, the editor of local English daily *The Sangai Express*: 'What empowerment? Do you know that many of these women sit with their vegetables, fish or other wares all day without selling anything? Or that at the end of the day they sell their goods at throwaway prices because they have to catch the last bus home? If they are late, they are beaten up by their husbands and often accused of having an affair. They also have to be in time to cook dinner for the family. Often their husbands snatch away their day's earnings!'

A woman selling dried fish looks at me and cries, 'Fifty rupees only. You won't find a better bargain.' Her gaze is full of appeal and I finally understand the import of the comment made by Rajesh Hijam that day.

⁓

I glance at my cellphone to check the time. I don't remember when I stopped wearing a wristwatch. It is nearly noon and I get up, 'Can anyone tell me where Ima Mutum Ibemhal's stall is? I am looking for her.' Everyone appears to know her. She is a celebrity, one among the brave women who took part in the historic nude protest. Sarita points out, 'Take a turn at that corner. Look for Shop No. 22.'

I get up and make my way across the crowd of screaming vendors and a colourful maze of shops filled with women haggling with buyers. Quite suddenly I stumble upon Shop 22, the number written on a copper plaque and hung carelessly on a top rail of the shop's wooden shutters. One cannot miss it, a one-stop store holding within its walls an eclectic collection of all items that are obligatory when a baby is born in a Meitei household – from items for Savasti Puja that celebrates the birth of a child, to tiny home-made silk mattresses, pillows, mosquito nets, steel bowls and plates, and an assorted array of pressure cookers, flasks, hurricane lamps and more. Occupying place of pride on its shelves is assorted imported merchandise from Moreh, the Indo-Myanmar trading point.

Shop No. 22 is a popular destination not only because of its collection, but also because it is graced by the warm presence of Ima Ibemhal, an affectionate grandmother. Ima Ibemhal informs me, 'Savasti Puja is very significant. The baby's maternal relatives visit in a procession, the women wear saffron phaneks and white *chadars* or white silk shawls, and carry presents in round baskets. The baskets are stuffed with *muri laddoos* (sweets made of puffed rice and jaggery), fish and clothes for both the child and the mother. The men follow the women and when they reach the house, *kirtans* are sung with the mother and the baby sitting around the *tulsi* plant which is found in every Meitei household.'

❧

I am intrigued by the institution of the *keithel* or market and the role it plays in the lives of the women of Manipur. For them, it is more than merely a source of livelihood: the marketplace creates bonds that are akin to blood ties. Although there are no written historical records, the common belief is that Ima Keithel dates back to colonial times and was christened after the Imas who manage it. There is also a story that traces the origin of the market's name to Goddess Ima, the female deity who presides over it.

As I look across at the crowded *keithal* from Ima Mutum Ibemhal's shop, I am dazzled. Someone appears to have dyed it in a riot of colours and in the many hues, I can glimpse charming vignettes of Manipur. Images of traditional handlooms and handicrafts, trinkets and grocery, home-grown vegetables, fresh fish and dried fish – all soak into my mind and I feel a strong sense of what one might call the essence of all things native to the land seeping into my mind. I send up a small prayer of gratitude for this small gift that will stay in my memory for a long time.

For the Imas who gather here every day to sell their wares, this is all routine: but for me or any other visitor, it is a lesson in kinship and fortitude. The violence, bloodshed, curfews and *bandhs* that define contemporary Manipur have left deep scars on Ima Market, you can see the toll they've taken in some of the faces, ravaged, sometimes oddly listless. But there's a way in which, the women have remained buoyant against the odds, drawing strength from their affinity for each other and striding ahead with tenacity of purpose. 'We suffer when there are prolonged conflicts. But we have homes and hearths to look after,' pronounces the Ima.

❧

Ima Ibemhal is '70-something'. 'I don't know my exact age,' she guffaws. Clad in traditional attire, with a handloom fabric cellphone case hanging around her neck, Ima Mutum Ibemhal is a picture of dignity and grace. Her specialty is her personal touch, evident in her kindly interactions with customers. She creates custom products for infants, and young mothers bank on her wisdom to source the most desirable things for their newborns.

Proudly displaying an exquisitely embroidered mattress made at the embroidery centre that she has at home, she says, 'I ensure that every product is of the best quality. I have grandchildren and value the emotions a child inspires.' It is this wisdom that inspires a sense of trust in customers, drawing them from far and wide. This gives her shop a special place in Ima Market.

I wait until her customers have all left before I ask her what prompted her to take part in the historic nude protest of 15 July 2004.

It is a lazy afternoon and the buzz of the market has eased a bit. Ima sits on a low stool on an elevated platform inside the shop and, leaning contentedly against the wall, peels off the layers of her remarkable life. I listen, rapt.

She has had to struggle to keep the shop. She had to learn to cope on her own when her husband died. In 1985, while still a young man, he was involved in a freak accident that affected his mental balance and he committed suicide. He was the one who had helped her set up Shop No. 22 back in August 1975; the store became her sole source of strength and succour when she became a widow.

Ima comes from an poor family. She dropped out of the Iboton Sana Girls High School, Imphal when she was in Class seven or eight, and was married off at the age of 15. After her husband's death, she took charge of the embroidery shop that her husband used to run with the help of an associate. These days, it is her son who looks after the shop, although the Ima makes sure to drop in for a few hours every day.

A mother of four daughters and three sons, who are all married, Ima now has seven homes. She visits and stays with each of her children in turn, happy that there is no permanent abode. 'My grandchildren always demand that I spend more time with them and I enjoy telling them bedtime stories. They are extremely fond of me and this love has helped me brave all storms and emerge smiling,' she pronounces with pride.

❧

Somewhere between the quiet pace of a small town and the noisy bustle of a metropolis is the city of Imphal. It is a pleasant enough urban space, although the sight of armed security personnel everywhere creates a deep sense of unease. The disquiet is obvious inside Ima Market too. The women who collect here to sell their wares are alive to the strife in the state, an unrest that has infiltrated into all of their lives, causing intense economic and social turmoil.

News spreads fast here and it is routine for Ima Ibemhal to listen to tales of torture, murder, killing, rape – these are part and parcel of life in Manipur. In the early 1980s, Ima could barely even remember the acronym AFSPA. Gradually, she learnt that it stands for the Armed Forces (Special Powers) Act, 1958 and grew wise to its many implications. Extended conversations with the other women in the market gave her insights into the problems that plague Manipur and also to the draconian Act. Her own life was touched by the violence when her older son, Tarun Singh, was abducted by the army and tortured so brutally that it left him with a permanent psychiatric problem, and her with a perennial scar in her life. In 1995, she was jailed for going on a hunger strike to protest the disappearance of a boy who had been picked up by the security forces.

In Ima Market, Ibemhal has earned a place of distinction. She is one of the mothers who participated in the iconic Kangla protest against the inhuman killing of Thangjam Manorama by security forces. 'You cannot miss her shop and her smile. We are proud that she is one of us here,' says Anima who owns a stall close to hers.

Besides being an active member of the Meira Paibi of her *leikai*, Ibemhal is also a social worker. She has been the President of the 'All Manipur Tammi (valley)-Chingmi (hill) Apunba Lup'. There are several such groups who work and share ideas about how to work towards a peaceful co-existence between the people of the valley and those of the hills of Manipur. In July 2004, Manorama's rape and killing shook her to the core and she went to the crucial 14 July meeting at Macha Leima. She was convinced that only an extraordinary protest would make the world sit up and take notice. She had felt impelled to reach out to billions of women around the world, make them realize what was happening in Manipur, how women were suffering as soft targets. 'It was acceptable even if I died while doing this; but I had to make people sit up and take notice of our plight. I was ready to die like a heroine – for a cause,' she remembers.

And a heroine she truly was. For her, the day of protest was not an ordinary one: it was a day of communion with God.

She had come to the market and opened her shop as usual. No one at home had any clue about what she had in mind. A few of her close friends in Ima Market knew and tried to dissuade her. They also expressed misgivings about her ability to participate in something as unusual and out of the ordinary as a nude protest. But she gave them no heed – her mind was already made up.

Ima Ibemhal did not flinch for a second when the protest was staged. Her primary concern was the brutality with which Manorama had been raped and killed. 'A message had to be delivered to the world. Manorama's rape and killing was an assault on the dignity of women in Manipur and should never ever recur,' she tells me.

On 15 July 2004, she had felt she was doing something propitious for her motherland. She had arrived at the Macha Leima office, taken off her gold earrings and bangles and after wrapping them in a piece of cloth, taken off her inner garments as well.

Many Imas had gone to the Kangla that day, but only 12 had stepped forward to disrobe. Ima Ibemhal remembers being totally engrossed in the protest and shouting 'Indian Army Rape Us' at the top of her voice. She also remembers having fainted because of the anxiety and stress and being taken to the J N Hospital.

Chitra Devi Chongtham, Ima Ibemhal's youngest daughter who also owns a shop in Ima Market, comes to join in our conversation. She is followed by Ima's second daughter, Thangjam Chaya, who also runs a shop in the marketplace. For both of them, memories flood in as they hear their mother speak about that 'agonizing day'. Chitra becomes emotional, recalling how her brother had called her to inform them that their mother had been hospitalized: 'Curfew had been declared and I could not go to the hospital. I felt helpless. But, I am proud that my mother could do something like this for the daughters of Manipur. I don't think I would have had the nerve to do it.'

Chaya quips, 'I was pained by the torment that caused my mother and the other Imas to even think about demonstrating in such an extraordinary way. The enaphi and the phanek are extremely significant for Manipuri women and the enaphi, worn by married women, is very difficult to take off.'

After her release from hospital, Ima Ibemhal went back to a still and quiet home. Nobody asked her any questions, nor did she proffer any explanation. She laughs, 'I did hear my sons telling their wives how embarrassing it was to go out of their homes, but they did not have the courage to say anything to me.'

Today, the people of the neighbourhood look up to Ima. She is everyone's mother. Her family allows her to do whatever she wants. Even today, if there is a protest march and she is late, her children go and look for her in the hospital. They are filled with pride when their mother is featured in newspapers and in photo exhibitions. Her grandchildren jump up in delight when they see her in the media.

Only Ima knows how meaningless it all is. Nothing has happened even after poets have composed verses and journalists and writers have written paeans of praise on the Mothers' Protest. Peace is fragile and she worries about the future of Manipur. She would never want her daughters to be compelled to stage a nude protest.

The irreverence of security forces, young men, born of mothers like her, angers her. 'Without Imas they can't exist,' she says. She is proud of Kangla, which she feels identifies their culture. It hurts her that the tradition of our ancestors had been occupied by the army. In 2004, Prime Minister Manmohan Singh fulfilled the persistent demand of the people of Manipur and announced that the Kangla Fort, which was occupied by the Assam Rifles, would be evacuated. She feels that it's a big achievement for them.

'I wish they would develop some kind of respect for women and children. I hope that the decision-makers think about revoking the dreaded AFSPA,' she says. She checks her mobile phone for any missed calls. Her eye wanders, her attention shifting to another customer. As the Ima engages with the new buyer, I feel it's time for me to leave. I smile at her and walk away.

2

Ngaithem Ningol Thokchom Ongbi Ramani Devi, aka Ima Ramani

People often respond to conflict in surprising and positive ways. Unlike his peers, a young civil engineering graduate from NIT, Patna in Bihar decided to move away from the comfortable clubs of the elite. He came back to his hometown, Imphal, and set up a war museum.

A resident of Tera Amudon Akham Leikei, a locality in Imphal, Arambam Angamba Singh, 42, opted to curate the Imphal War Museum to showcase the relics of World War II. He is the co-founder of World War II Imphal Campaign Foundation, which aims to promote and preserve the rich heritage of the Battle of Imphal, which is also known as Britain's Greatest Battle of all time by the National Army Museum in UK. The keen enthusiast began by using a bare room at his own house as a temporary location. Gradually, support flowed in – the Manipur government allocated a heritage building for the museum and the Japanese government also collaborated in the project.

I have seen many history buffs in Manipur. Setting up museums by individuals is not unusual. Several years ago, I had met a fascinating self-taught man, Mutua Bahadur, who had set up several museums – a museum of arts and crafts in Imphal, a cultural complex for the preservation of the material heritage of the region's Andro village, some 26 kilometres from Imphal, and a 'living museum' at Purul village in Senapati district to preserve the carved houses of different tribes.

It's not often that parents encourage their qualified sons to do something as difficult as setting up a museum. However, Arambam's parents and wife are supportive of his choice. It's not surprising because he was born and raised in a house stacked with war books, thanks to his army man father. He was fascinated by the sepia-tinted black and white photographs of Imphal and Kohima during the battle period and would flip through them a thousand times. Many stories are passed down from his elders. His paternal grandmother spoke of the Goras (the British), the Japanese air raids, the Z-shaped air raid trenches and how they used to take shelter with a lantern and bushel of pounded rice; she told him about hiding Japanese soldiers in the granary, fleeing Imphal during the raids and about hiding her dowry in the pond, never to be found again when they returned.

I confess that I have little knowledge about the

war. Arambam is patient with my queries. He has just come back after a whirlwind tour with a Japanese war enthusiast. He sits me down and gives me a brief history of the war. Imphal, the capital city of Manipur which lies in the easternmost corner of India, bordering Burma, or present day Myanmar, was a key battleground during the Second World War. A remote outpost of the Raj until then, in 1942, it suddenly found itself on the frontier between Japanese-occupied Burma and the British in India. It turned into a major Second World War battlefield in 1944 when the Japanese, together with Indian National Army (INA) units, invaded India.

In describing the hostilities of 1944, Arambam quotes British military historian Robert Lyman who describes as 'climactic' and 'titanic' the impact and reality of the terrible war that raged across the jungle-clad hills. Indeed, the battles near Imphal and in Kohima in neighbouring Nagaland are seen as the turning point in what came to be known as the Burma Campaign. This campaign saw not just the Japanese invasion of India repelled, but ultimately reversed, with the Allies subsequently driving them out of Burma and beyond. The Japanese lost 49,000 men in what was one of their single greatest military defeats. According to Lyman, 'It is clear that Kohima/Imphal was one of the four great turning-point battles in the Second World War, when the tide of war changed irreversibly and dramatically against those who initially held the upper hand.' The battles at Stalingrad, El Alamein and in the Pacific are the other three.

As I chat with him, I feel as if I am flipping through the pages of a history book. Arambam reminds me why the war was a momentous period in Manipur's history. In a few short years, Manipur's infrastructure was developed like never before and its population exposed to the presence of tens of thousands of soldiers from different parts of India and the world. 'The impact of this war had a tremendous effect on our society as Manipur came in touch with various nationalities like the British, Americans, Africans, Pathans, Japanese and so on,' he explains.

Manipur saw a great deal of hardship during World War II. But in a way, the war leapfrogged the state from a 19th century civilization to a 20th century one. Road connectivity from Dimapur to Imphal improved with the construction of an all-weather road, and the airstrip at Koirengei was used for civilian flights till another airstrip built during World War II at Tulihal was converted into the present Imphal airport. As Arambam points out, 'The use of motor vehicles became common for various purposes leading to economic changes. If the war had not been fought in Manipur, the present level of development would not have been achieved'.

Arambam was lucky because he found a friend who shared his passion for museums. 'While I was collecting and researching the battle of Imphal I met this friend with similar interests with whom I co-founded the Foundation. My passion grew. I wanted to unravel the history of the battle. We then started identifying important landmarks, battle sites and vital facts on a regular basis.'

Most memories associated with a war are sad and painful. However, Arambam's perception of the war is different. He is pained that his people are not aware of the value of these relics and that they are not concerned that these valuable things might be lost. This made him even more determined to set up a war museum. 'The objective is not the glorification of the war but the connection that you get when you actually see the things with your own eyes,' he says.

He and his associate conduct battle tours regularly. They are the first members of the UK-based International Guild of Battlefield Guides in Asia. 'It is also our duty to preserve and safeguard this important chapter in the history of Manipur,' he says. A large part of the display has come from donations from families and relatives. They also do excavations of battle sites on a regular basis.

But any war leaves behind its scars. The battles in 1944 are also said to have cost the people dear: many had to evacuate their homes and seek shelter elsewhere; villages were bombed and houses destroyed during some of the most intense moments of the fighting. 'Manipur with a population of slightly above five lakhs, hosted a combined troop strength of 1.5 lakh and from this one can visualise the impact it must have on the local population.'

Though a generation apart, Arambam's war museum reflects the early life of Ima Ramani, who grew up during World War II and was one of the mothers who took part in the nude protest at Kangla. As a child, when the battle was going on, little Ramani's cherished game was 'Bomb, Bomb'. She and her friends would start running if one of them blew a whistle. Another would pretend to be an airplane and a third would dive for cover, leaping into a small trench they had dug with a spade borrowed from her mother's small kitchen garden.

She learnt this when they were in Singjemai in Imphal where they had to run for cover to survive bombings from the Japanese airplanes. The trenches too were not safe as often there were snakes and insects inside them. The sound of falling bombs felt like thunderclaps. Her family was a part of the phenomenon called 'Japan Ianchenba' or running away from the Japan war, where people of Imphal ran away to different villages.

Life at their makeshift home at Thoubal was difficult. She knew there was no food to eat and her mother was trying to prepare *heikrak*, also known as water chestnut. Scientifically, it belongs to the trapa species. Resembling the samosa, it grows in bunches and its soft, hollow stem is a delicacy in Manipur. It is seldom cooked and is generally had raw as part of a salad. Her mother used to finish cooking early before it got dark as there was no electricity and no kerosene to light the lamp. Everything had to be over before dusk set in else one had to grope in the dark. There was a scarcity of rice and salt and everything was very expensive. There were no plates and they had to eat on banana or cabbage leaves.

She recalls how her family trudged the stretch from Singjemei Thongam Leikai to Thoubal. Often, she was too tired to walk and her mother carried her on her back. It was almost a 20 kilometre distance. She was some eight or nine years old and was in the second grade and had to quit school then. She often participated in a cultural programme called Sanjenba, which is based on the life of the god Krishna, and describes his birth, his childhood and his youth.

'The Japanese soldiers used to play with the children during the day, but at night they would knock on the door and ask for young girls. There's a strange kind of similarity with the present day situation in Manipur. Every mother was paranoid about the safety of her daughters,' she says. Her childhood was full of struggle – there are no happy memories. No good stories, only heartbreaking ones. When things calmed down a bit, they came back, but had to flee again, this time to Wangoi, when the aerial bombings started anew.

This little girl grew up, got married and like most Meitei women, got actively involved in social work. She runs an NGO, the All Manipur Social Development and Reformation Samaj, which fights against things like alcoholism and gambling. A reformist at heart, Ramani feels that the young minds need to be guided in order to create an ideal society. 'It so happened that my son who is active in the local community clubs, used to organize functions. In one such function, a drunkard created a nuisance and there was a big quarrel. The local people came forward to beat him.' The incident inspired her to start working against alcoholism and try to convince young people to stay away from it.

Ramani's tryst with the war zone she was born in is far from over.

It was getting dark as we sat on the stairs of the verandah of the newly constructed part of her house. I could see a rather old and battered car parked in the garage. Its white paint had yellowed with age, and it was covered with patches. Inside, there was no electricity. Her sparse living room looked a bit ghostly in the half light. The walls held photographs of political leaders, including Sonia Gandhi. And at one side, there was a red refrigerator with a voltage stabilizer sitting on top.

Ramani's is a typical Meitei household. She lives in an east-facing house with a courtyard in front and a tulsi plant in the middle. There are other houses adjacent to it, also facing east. She has a big family – three sons and three daughters. Her youngest son passed away a while back. She also has grandchildren – six grandsons and three granddaughters. As we talked, a petite young girl came and sat with us. Ima introduced her as her granddaughter, Th. Mamta who was studying in Chennai. She sat with us and helped her grandmother recall her past by giving her leads. Obviously she'd heard Ramani's stories before.

It's almost as if Ima Ramani enters a time warp and begins to tell us about some lesser known slices of Manipur's history. Men, women and children, all part of her family, come out and watch and listen as she starts speaking. A few women sit near her and cut vegetables and prepare to cook dinner.

Almost instinctively, she tries to cover her ankle and feet with her phanek. Traditionally when the phanek is worn it is supposed to hide even the feet of a woman. If a woman wears the phanek above her feet, she is considered high-handed. She feels uneasy even when it's pulled up slightly. She is also very particular about the upper garment, the enaphi. So much so, she even covers herself when she goes to sleep.

Her husband sits quietly on a wooden armchair in the courtyard, occasionally giving us a curious look. He is bare-chested with a *Khudei* (a printed loin cloth used as a cotton handwoven towel) tied around his waist. 'He does not speak much. He's not keeping well either,' she tells us. She tells me that her husband used to play a musical instrument called 'climat' in a band at marriages and on other happy occasions. 'Climat?' I ask, looking baffled. She raises her voice with a mischievous smile as she explains, 'He played a long instrument, like you blow a horn.' Her granddaughter smiles and corrects her, 'She's talking of the clarinet.' Ramani smiles and adds in a matter-of-fact manner, 'Yes, whatever.' She then tells me more about her husband. Later he was employed as a compounder in a hospital. Now he is leading a retired life. 'I am his second wife. He has no contact with his first wife,' she adds.

Ramani is also a good traditional dancer and has worked in the traditional courtyard theatre known as Shumang Leela. These are plays where women's roles are enacted by men. She's also formed an All Women Shumang Leela group. She says there's nothing unusual about this. A group of women got together and they decided to do it. But they did manage to break a long-established norm. She became a big hit for her role of Nongban (a villain) in the legendary love story of Khamba Thoibi. In fact, her husband too became a big fan of the play. And she has won several state level awards. He encouraged her and accompanied her when she went to other places to perform.

All these accomplishments notwithstanding, she is now much better known for the famous Kangla protest. It was not an easy decision for her. But, as she said, this time round, she listened to her heart. The brutal molestation and death of Manorama shook her as she felt it was a violation of the dignity of the women of Manipur. As she narrates the events of the fateful day, she says, 'It was almost like the last day of my life. It was such a difficult decision that I did not think that I would be alive after that. Such a protest should not happen again. If it has to recur, it will destroy the reputation of all Manipuri women.'

The night before the protest was unyielding. She could not sleep. She was filled with apprehension about the fallout of the protest. 'There were no second thoughts. We simply banged the gates of Kangla inviting the Assam Rifles to kill us and rape us,' she says.

She says the security personnel have no respect for women in society. This is why there is no point wearing clothes. 'By stripping, we wanted to deliver a message – you can see whatever you want and for as long as you want.' The women had decided that on principle, stripping was almost as good as dying. 'The government never tried to understand the heart of the mothers,' she tells me, with tears in her eyes.

She did not tell her family what she was going to do. The secret was not easy to keep. The women had decided on a protest that would be singular and unprecedented in the history of Manipur. They were unsure what would happen. The decision was taken to make people aware of the pain of the people of Manipur and unite against the AFSPA. And Kangla Fort was the ideal destination as the perpetrators were stationed there at the time.

She agrees that it is not a joke to stage a protest of this kind. The women did a small puja before they removed their inner clothes. Wrapped only in the phanek and enaphi, they reached the place and looked at each other. Kangla is a considered a sacred place and these women prayed to God when they saw Kangla.

She grew up against the backdrop of terror, though her immediate family did not have to face any violence. She tells me the story of a housewife called Prabhahini who was in bed under a mosquito net with her small baby when the army rushed in and shot her down. A theatre artiste, I. Mangi Jogendra was killed on the way back from rehearsal. Once there was an incident of firing near her house when a volleyball match was going on and CRPF shot dead 14 spectators. 'I tried to help the injured and my clothes were drenched with blood,' she recalls.

On the day of the protest she was numb, devoid of any feelings. None of the women informed their families. When she realized what she had done, she felt a sense of shame. But she was also happy that the security personnel did not dare to look at them. She was among the few women who fainted. She also worried about how her family and neighbours would react. Th. Kiran Kumar, her son who is a government servant, saw the protest on television. 'I was stunned but also proud. I wanted my mother to achieve her goal,' he says.

After the protest, Ramani thought that this was probably the ultimate protest against the Act. But to her dismay, the state of affairs has not improved. Initially the women had hoped that there would be some amendment to the Armed Forces (Special Powers) Act. They felt their act of stripping had the impact of building solidarity against the Act among the common people. She was convinced that she and her co-protestors had taken the right decision, but was disappointed at how little they had achieved.

Manipur hasn't changed much since then. Even today, protests, flaming tyres, teargas shells are a common sight. It's very common that people are picked up and then reported killed in an encounter. 'The authorities seem apathetic to the sufferings of Manipur. We don't want big buildings but peace. Let them repeal the Act and then the situation will slowly normalise.'

She says that if the situation remains like this, a time will come when there will be no men left in Manipur. 'I don't want another Nupi Lan, but if things continue like this – security forces keep killing innocents, we might have one.'

Dusk sets in and I have to strain my eyes to see her. She suddenly rises, as if she has remembered an important task. She checks on her husband to make sure he is fine. She puts a light shawl over him. She sighs, 'I don't think much now. But I sometimes feel that the protest was futile. Maybe it will be a legend for the future generations. We have probably become part of history books and museums.'

3

Ima Soibam Momon, aka Ima Momon:
Hardships in Verse

It was past midnight
The goddess of Delhi city
Wide eyed, sharp nosed is in her slumber
Roving my eyes for passers by, I pushed
The tall, long, God-like
Qutub Minar
Thought I can't do without taking it to Imphal
I fancied Qutub Minar standing by the Samu Makhong
(a historic sculpture in Manipur)

– Qutub Minar, a song originally in Meitei, written by
leading Manipur rock band Imphal Talkies

This song is about an insomniac young man from
Manipur, who studies and stays in India's capital city,
New Delhi, and is so disillusioned by the way things are
going in his home state because of the Armed Forces
(Special Powers) Act that has been in place there for

many years, that he rips off the Qutub Minar and takes it all the way to Manipur. The song is satirical and it narrates the journey of this man through Bihar, Assam, Nagaland and Manipur with the Qutub Minar. Towards the end of the song, the chief minister of Manipur says that the central government is crumbling as the opposition party has claimed that Prime Minister Manmohan Singh has gifted the Qutub Minar to the President of the USA, Barack Obama. Things become more charged as the adamant man tries to bargain with the government. He says that the centre can have the Qutub Minar back only if they repeal the draconian AFSPA, 1958 from Manipur. But before he gives it back, he will carve all the names of the Manipuri victims of AFSPA on the monument.

Sachidananda, the guitarist of the band tells me, 'The man is a symbolic figure of the thousands of disillusioned youths from the state who go to the mainland and try to blend in, but then somehow they end up realizing that they are different. Everyone relates to the guy with the Qutub Minar in one way or the other, I relate to that man in my own way. I like his farcical and satirical way of narrating things.' Sachidananda studied English literature in Dayanand Anglo Vedic College in Chandigarh and later did his post graduation from Punjab University. The song also reflects the fact that for most of India, Manipur is nothing more than a hazy geo-political riddle in a remote corner.

Injured is an inner state of being in Manipur. After

angry protests and agitations, it is music and poetry that are emerging as powerful modes of expressing therapeutic anger for many in this bullet-riddled state. 'Would you mind if I ask you a few questions?' I ask Sachidananda. 'Depending on what you ask,' the young musician responds. At my request, he begins to tell me the story of his journey into the world of contemporary music.

'I am not much of a musician. I've had no formal training. But I have loved music since childhood. I started playing the guitar when I was in the eleventh grade in school. Later, I joined some rock bands during my college days in DAVC, Chandigarh.' It's in music that he seeks solace whenever he is sad, 'I think music is magical. Every time I am low or depressed I wish I had a guitar with me. With a guitar I try to create new tunes and I'm so happy at the end of each session.' Now, he tries to balance academics and music as he is doing his PhD from Manipur University.

Talking about Manipur's very own Pete Seger, Akhu Chingangbam, the founder and lyricist and singer of Imphal Talkies, Sachidananda says, 'I see him as a poet with a guitar. I just add some music, that's all.' He explains the genesis of the band. It started very casually. He was friends with Akhu. One fine day in 2008, Akhu told him that he wanted to record some songs and would like him to play. He played the guitar in eight songs and they cut the album called 'Tidim Road'.

It is difficult not to admire Akhu's chutzpah. With a post-doctoral degree in Cosmology from Naresuan University, Phitsanulok, Thailand, he is a former student of physics and a full-time musician now. 'Sometimes I wish my PhD degree was just a tube guitar amplifier,' he says on Facebook. 'Bomb me, I am done collecting broken pieces of myself,' is another Facebook status update I came across. Most of my interactions with Akhu have been through social media, since it's easier to meet him in cyberspace. When I meet him offline, Akhu is quiet but sharp. He doesn't seem to care how he looks, or what others think of him. He sings about contemporary Manipur, and feels that eulogizing the rich culture and tradition of Manipur is not for him. 'There are guns pointed at you all the time. I feel life is too short not to sing all that I see. Our roots have gone out and taken up somewhere else. I want to be contemporary and talk about my generation.' 'Eche' (elder sister) is a song he wrote, which he recorded with his band mate Sachin in 2010, as a tribute to Irom Sharmila completing ten years of her protest fast against the AFSPA.

The name of the band, Imphal Talkies, dates back to his growing years. 'It was one of the theatres I used to go often with friends as an adolescent. We went there because there you could get to see 'A' rated movies. When I remember those days I think how innocent we were then, something I don't see at all any more in Manipur today. Also musically, I want my music to represent Imphal, the talking Imphal that speaks of its good and bad.'

Akhu and his team are now engaged in a new project – to use music as a therapeutic tool in collaboration with an NGO called Foundation for Social Transformation (FST). In this project, they will be working with two orphanages in Imphal that shelter orphans of conflict, and impart music lessons to them. The project aims to provide a creative outlet to release the trauma people have lived with through music. They hope to come up with a music album containing songs written, composed and performed by these kids. These children, from different castes, tribes and religion are bound by a common thread of having lost everything to conflict.

Akhu's music, amidst the debris of burnt houses, daily frisking, humiliation, curfews, random arrests and the stench of funeral pyres, took me back to Ima Momon's shimmering eyes as she spoke of her eldest son, another revolutionary poet and the pivot of her life. The painful reality of life under the draconian laws like the Armed Forces (Special Powers) Act, 1958 stirred her eldest son, Konungjao, alias Paikhomba, to write revolutionary stories, ditties and songs. Every year, he composes a song called 'Ima Pukkei' and records it on a CD called 'Poknaphan Ima' (Our Motherland). He's been composing new songs for the past five years.

He writes about contemporary Manipur. He usually writes in the dead of night, when the world is asleep. He never recites the poem to anyone before it is published. 'He is married with two kids. His wife is a housewife, she stitches mosquito nets and does tailoring to add to the family income. But I fear for his life. I am anxious all the time,' says Momon.

It has become a ritual for Momon and her family every year. Every time her defiant son releases his CD, army men come to his house, blindfold him and take him to some unknown place and mentally harass and beat him. And the family members go and convince the authorities that he is a harmless and peace loving citizen of the state. The poems are just an emotional outburst, a reflection of his understanding of the situation in the state and an expression of his deep feelings. One of his poems which stirred Momon, is titled 'Long Live the boundary of Manipur'. She glows with pride as she says, 'Now he is becoming famous and I encourage him to continue writing.' The local music companies have now recognized his talent and invite him to write songs. When asked to sing a song written by her son, Momon smiles and says, 'I can't sing.'

The next time I meet Momon is in a different setting. It's past 8 pm. A 68-year-old portly grandmother is getting ready to retire for the night. Her name, Momon, means 'soft', and she has chubby cheeks and a genial smile. As she smiles, one can see her lips are red and the red of the paan she is chewing touches her teeth too. Chewing a little bit of betel nut or *kwa chaba* is common in Manipur after lunch or dinner. Momon has finished with her puja and has a flower stuck behind her ear.

But she is not within the safe confines of her home. There are no grandchildren waiting to cuddle her. She has 13 grandchildren from her three daughters and three sons. When I meet her this time round, she is with her Meira Paibi friends and they are getting ready to sleep in the makeshift tent at the Planning and Development Agency (PDA) complex at Porompat in Imphal East. She has been engaged in the relay hunger strike called 'Save Sharmila, Repeal AFSPA' since 10 December 2008 which is also the Day of the Universal Declaration of Human Rights. I look at her gold chain with a triangular pendant that stands out in the austere ambience, with the banner behind her that proclaims, 'Relay Hunger Strike'.

The women have brought their own bed rolls and mats. The place looks like a makeshift dormitory where they lay their mats on the floor and make their beds. Some of them are busy in the 'kitchen' they've cobbled together, which is separated by a bamboo wall. They will have an early dinner of rice and *iromba* (a curry made with fermented fish) and then sit and chat. They are in a world of their own – away from the pressures of domesticity and mundane household chores. They talk about their lives, their families, their society and their dilemmas.

She is a Meira Paibi first. And that is her prime concern. The Meira Paibi (torch bearers) movement is a fairly recent women's movement in Manipur which comprises many older women. There are Meira Paibi groups operating in all localities. They came into being in the 1970s with the Nishabandh movement, when women decided to deal with the menace of alcoholism and drunken and often violent husbands, and also to try to keep young people away from liquor and drugs.

Meira Paibis are present in every Meitei locality in Manipur. They are an insurance against human right violations and social evils. They keep vigil with torches in their hands for 3-4 hours every night in their locality. They have devised a system of clanging two poles whenever there is danger or a problem and the moment they hear this they rush out of their homes. The collective spirit of the women binds them together and also instils fear in the hearts of anti-social elements. The women raise their voices whenever there are cases of atrocities by the security forces and they take part in rallies and dharnas. The 28th of May is observed as Meira Paibi day in the state.

Ima Momon is a proud Meira Paibi. Wife of a retired schoolteacher, she is an activist in her own right. She is the co-convenor of the Sharmila Apunba Lup, an organization set up to support Irom Sharmila in her hunger strike against AFSPA, and president of the All Manipur Tammi-Chingmi Apunba Nupi Lup. And her family doesn't mind if she spends nights outside in a tent. 'I have three daughters-in-law to take care of the house,' she smiles. She got involved in the ways of the world quite early: she studied only till class 8 and married at the early age of 14.

She remembers growing up in a tranquil Manipur. As a child, Momon was very hardworking. She was involved in school activities, particularly sports and traditional dance. At home, she used to weave and spin. Her mother was a strict disciplinarian. She was allowed to eat only when she finished her weaving for the day. She grew up before her age.

She remembers how, in those days, they were not allowed to go the main market alone even though the situation was quite peaceful. 'It was only after the merger agreement [in 1949 when the princely state of Manipur became part of India] that atrocities started. The state became violent and bloody,' she tells me.

Like any mother, Ima Momon has one nagging worry. Her second son is an alcoholic and she has been urging him to give up drinking. To help, she found him a job selling newspapers. In the beginning, Momon's husband was reluctant to support her in her social activities; he thought she was wasting her time, and her elder son supported the father. But Ima Momon managed to convince them otherwise.

Ima Momon is one of the few protestors who knew Thangjam Manorama personally. The Manorama she knew was a young punctilious girl who used to collect handloom materials from the weavers' houses and sell them in the market. She did not know the Manorama who was 'allegedly' an explosives expert and belonged to a militant group. She knew a Manorama who was the sole breadwinner of her family.

Ima Momon was deeply distressed by the way she was killed. Manorama was raped and tortured in the verandah of her house. Water was poured through her nose and her clothes were slashed. The police claim she was shot as she was trying to run. 'There were seven bullet bores in her private parts. Why did the bullet not hit her from the back if she was running away?' Momon was in the hospital when the post-mortem was being conducted. After seeing Manorama's mutilated body, she resolved to do something that would ensure that this terrible act never be repeated.

Initially they had planned a massive rally on 16 July 2004. But the government announced curfew on that day. So they came up with an alternative plan on 15 July. A group of Imas vowed that they would strip themselves. 'There is no respect for mothers and sisters in our society. There is no point in wearing clothes at all,' she says.

When she stood in front of the Kangla gate, she was nervous about whether she would have the courage to take the step they had planned. Would she really be able to do it? But suddenly, the tears started falling and she found herself unbuttoning her blouse. After she had stripped fully, instead of feeling a sense of shame, she felt stronger. Shaking the iron gates and screaming 'Come and rape us' made her feel powerful. She could not see anything other the huge iron gates and a blurred image of Manorama's body deep in her consciousness.

Right after the protest, the commandos came looking for the Imas. Ima Momon went into hiding for nearly three months. She was even arrested under NSA once. But she is undeterred. She laughs when she says that there are times when the police come and ask her husband about her. Her husband expresses his helplessness by saying, 'She has already dedicated her life to the cause of her motherland. I don't know anything about her.'

Ima Momon and her friends are determined to fight against all 'evils' – from alcoholism to 'indecent frisking of women by security forces'. Raising their voice against the 'indecent' frisking by state women police during a combing operation at Khwairamband Keithel, more than half a dozen civil society organizations, mainly women's bodies, have warned the state government that they will launch an agitation if such things recur. Akhu sums up their agony in these poignant lines:

> *…This is my town*
> *I am the one who should be asking you*
> *about your identity!*
> *Don't stop me, I am late to find freedom.*
> *This is my town*
> *the streets carry my footmarks*
> *since I could walk*
> *no matter how dusty they are….*

Several years have gone by since the historic 'nude' protest. Ima Momon realizes, clichéd as it is, that while the wounds are deep, given time and distance, the scars will fade. She hopes perhaps someday everyone can walk tall. She does not forsee a rosy future for Manipur though. She wonders how fragile freedom and life are. Ten years down the line, she feels more and more lives have been lost. And it is the women who will become vulnerable. More people will die and cry. I look at Ima Momon and her associates who are fighting what sometimes seems like a futile battle, while Akhu and his band continue to sing poignant songs. Commenting on the mother's protest, Akhu says, 'I was not surprised actually. Manipur is a place where you have a woman who fasts for 14 years. Therefore, all forms of protests are expected as the level of injustice escalates.' This haunting melody from the Imphal Talkies seems to sum up the situation in Ima Momon's Manipur:

> ... *What is India doing to Sharmila*
> *They raped and killed Manorama*
> *No one remembers Chittaranjan*
> *Everyone saw it wide open*
> *The fools they shut down the schools*
> *Children they use like tools*
> *Me too, a son of that land and let me tell you your*
>   *institution is a lie.*

4

Ima Yumlembam Mema, aka Ima Mema

Manipur is full of opinions, angry discussions and incredibly touching stories. And I am always eager to listen. I sip tea and munch on thin arrowroot biscuits, as 32-year-old Lucy Khumlo tells me her tale. She is from Manipur's Chandel district. I listen as she talks, 'The village church is the most sacred place for me. Whenever I am distressed, I go and sit in the church and find solace.'

I see her eyes moisten as she recalls the fateful day when she and her three children were left to sit all alone on a bench in the church. She could overhear offensive remarks by her friends and neighbours; the looks of disdain from the churchgoers tormented her. After her husband died of HIV-AIDS in 2003, she decided to start her life afresh. Dressed in her Sunday best, she had gone to the church with her children, only to be shunned.

As a young HIV-positive widow, Lucy's life took several twists and turns. She had acquired the virus from her husband, who was an Intravenous Drug User (IDU). Taunts from her in-laws got worse after she revealed her HIV status. They blamed her for their son's death. Lucy had an early marriage. She fell in love with the man who became her husband when she was a student of Class X. The young bride was unaware of the fact that her husband was an IDU. Now, even her 11-year-old HIV-positive daughter has been ostracized by her friends. Lucy is deeply distressed about this.

Alone and hurt, Lucy had to spend many restless nights. She then came in touch with the women's wing of the Imphal-based Manipur Network of Positive People (MNP+). They inspired her to come out of her depression. She pronounced her decision to go public about her HIV-positive status and educate other women like her. She started working for MNP+ as a peer educator and is now the Vice-President of the Chandel Network of Positive People.

She is one of the visible faces of the feminization of HIV-AIDS. She joined hands with a group of women living with HIV-AIDS. They decided to shed the shroud of secrecy and confront the stigma associated with the virus. Most of them are young widows in the age group of 16 to 25 years. Since the first HIV case, which was reported in Manipur in 1992, most husbands have died and later, their widows were tested positive. Of the 1600 members of MNP+, over 700 are women. Nearly 98 per cent of them contracted the disease from their husbands.

They are representative of the fact that married women in monogamous relationships are the new face of the epidemic.

Lucy's story took me thousands of miles away to a friendly luncheon at Heritage India located in Dupont Circle, Washington DC, where a new-fangled idea was brewing. Three powerful women – Leslie Wolfe, Jane Ransom and Yolonda Richardson – heads of three global women's organizations based in Washington DC namely the Centre for Women Policy Studies (CWPS), International Women's Media Foundation (IWMF) and Centre for Development and Population Activities (CEDPA) were toying with an idea. They wanted to steer an innovative sisterhood of women all over the world. And little did I realize that I would also be a part of it one day.

The lunch led to the birth of a new resolve – to chart a new course of partnership for women's rights, particularly among three sectors – parliamentarians, journalists and civil society actors – who rarely work together in a 'safe space'. Their first initiative was to foster a women-centered HIV/AIDS policy in India, Kenya and Mexico. Being part of this new sisterhood was an eye-opener for me. I had been reporting on Manipur and Nagaland for many years now, and I knew that the main source of HIV-AIDS in Manipur had been the Intravenous Drug Users (IDUs) and their 'needle-sharing' practices. This was due to the easy availability of drugs, as Manipur happens to be the transit route for narcotic drugs like heroin and marijuana because of its close proximity to the Golden Triangle, that is, Thailand, Laos and Myanmar. IDUs kicked off as a fashion among the unemployed, disillusioned youth in this insurgency-ravaged state.

As women from diverse countries, we found we faced similar problems. The interaction revealed that the new problem now was the alarming rise in HIV positive cases among married women in monogamous relationships. I meet the feisty activist Udita Salam, 40, who is also the general secretary of MNP+ and an IDU spouse, and she draws out the discrimination that women face. When men get sick, they get medical attention, support and nutrition from their family members. But after the man dies, the woman is driven out, ostracized and denied her property rights. And if she has acquired the virus, there is nobody to take care of her.

Udita describes the prevalent social norms. Most often, the woman is ignorant of the husband's IDU status. 'It invariably happens that these men are married off by their family members in the belief that after marriage, they will become responsible householders. The women later end up being homeless as they do not get property rights. There are no caregivers for women,' adds Udita.

She is herself a graduate who married an IDU in 1989. She thought that she would be able to change his behaviour post marriage. But alarm bells started ringing when her three-month old son died in 1997 and her positive status was confirmed. It was then that her husband admitted that he was HIV positive. Now, both of them work for MNP+.

Scars tend to linger and I keep rediscovering crusaders in Manipur again and again. Women of the Meira Paibis in every locality of Manipur are crusading against the menace of drug abuse and alcoholism. I set out to meet one such campaigner, Ima Mema, who had participated in the nude protest at Kangla.

A few bicycles rattle past as I gingerly walk the muddy path, trying to make my way to Ima Mema's house. The neighbourhood had contiguous sets of houses, securely barricaded by tall woven sheets of hollow bamboo. Most of the houses have a gate made of corrugated tin sheets with a pair of metal buckles to fix the lock. Till a few years back, insular houses with closed gates were rather unusual in a semi-urban locality like Wangkhei Thoubalkhong in Imphal East district. Little boys chase each other through the dusty backstreets and one of them trips and falls down and lets out a shrill cry. I pick him up and ask him the directions for Ima Mema's house. He points to the right and scurries off.

I knock at the tall tin gate and wait. Soon, a neatly dressed septuagenarian opens the door and warmly ushers me in. Attired in customary Meitei clothes, she has applied sandalwood paste on the bridge of the nose and carved an elongated quadrilateral mark. This is connected by two parallel lines reaching up to the forehead. She wears a rosary of tulsi beads, traditionally known as *Urik*, around her neck and a pair of gold earrings carved in a traditional design in her ears.

There isn't a streak of grey in her carefully combed hair which is neatly tied in a bun. I point to my own hair, peppered with grey and ask her the secret of her jet-black mane. Her forehead creases as she breaks into a wide smile. 'Of course, I dye my hair. I don't go to a beauty parlour like you young girls, but when people like you come to meet me, I have to look good. I have to be prim and proper,' she chuckles. I tell her, 'Of course, Ima. You are beautiful.' And we both burst into laughter.

She asks me to sit on a wooden chair in the verandah of her house. She mutters, 'Eeswar Leiri' (God is there). She kneels down on the ground which has been freshly scrubbed with cow dung, folds her hands and offers prayers to the Tulsi plant in the centre of the *shumang* (courtyard). Basil, also known as the 'King of herbs' is considered sacred and is an important component of every Meitei household. It is an essential part of many rites and rituals. It is a symbol of their adherence to the Vaishnavite faith. It's a daily ritual for her.

'One thing I ask for from God in all my prayers is the repeal of the oppressive AFSPA. This Act is the cause of all our other problems, including social evils like drug abuse and alcoholism which is destroying our youth,' she tells me.

She doesn't have the statistics but she knows that there are many IDUs in her neighbourhood. As per the National Aids Control Organisation (NACO) statistics, out of the 8 million IDUs in the world, as many as 20,000 are in Manipur and these drug users transmit the virus to their partners through sexual intercourse. 'I have seen many families suffer and many youngsters destroy themselves,' she says.

She makes herself comfortable in the verandah of her spartan house. Half of the wall is made of concrete and the other half with tin. Ima Mema explains that it's her daughter's house. Her husband, who was a mechanic, died early and she has been staying with her only daughter R. K. Mukta Sinha. She teaches English at Dameswari Junior High School. Her daughter was widowed 21 years ago. She has five grandchildren – four boys and one girl.

Ima Mema has been a close observer of Manipuri society over the years. AFSPA, the draconian legislation, is 50 years old and she is 70. In retrospect, she can see a lot of difference between the situation now and then. Now she misses the sense of freedom she enjoyed and the little pleasures of life she could savour when she was young.

She could study only till Class IX. As a child, she vaguely remembers the bombings during World War II. Her family members used to hide in the underground trenches whenever a plane overflew their house. She married early but, as she says, 'In those days, girls did not study much. If a girl wanted to do so, it was frowned upon,' she smiles.

But in today's Manipur, she feels there is fear all around. She too is frightened much of the time. She is scared for her granddaughter if she goes out alone. 'There was a time when women could go for late night shows in cinema halls and it was perfectly safe. Now things have come to such a pass that any family member who ventures out is cautioned to come back before dark,' she says.

And grandmothers like her are worried about their grandchildren. 'It's fairly common to see youths being killed in fake encounters now. The pattern is the same in media reports – a person killed and a grenade, or a gun found near him. It's a common belief that if a person is carrying more than Rs 1,000, he might be killed by the security forces,' she says, much to my astonishment.

Ima Mema is rather acerbic as she explains the grim scenario in her state. The commonly held belief is that corruption is so rampant in Manipur, that getting a sub-inspector's job means having to pay a bribe of Rs 1,500,000. And this for a salary of a mere Rs 12,000. Therefore, if someone is caught with Rs 7,000 during frisking, an easy option is to kill the person in a 'fake' encounter and snatch the money. 'I will not give more than Rs 500 to my grandson,' she says, grimly.

I listen, intrigued, as this wise grandmother describes

her community. 'An ancient proverb states that the Meitei community have eyes on their fingers. This implies that our community is extremely talented. If the population of the Meitei is reduced, it will be easier for the authorities to control them. It is a ploy to suppress a clever community,' she says. In the prevailing anarchic law and order situation, if things go on the way they are, she fears that there will be no men or youth left.

Ima Mema is very perceptive when it comes to drawing attention to their cause. She is sad that many outsiders come to document their stories but nothing really changes. 'Instead of publishing our stories in India, we should reach out to foreign shores and garner support for our cause,' she says.

When we begin talking about the Kangla protest, she sits back and closes her eyes. Her face is blank. I see her hands trembling. It was not difficult for her to strip, she says. The future of the youth of Manipur was constantly in her thoughts. She feels that the act of stripping, of exposing herself, was a deep loss of privacy and dignity. 'It was almost like raping oneself. Still the government has done nothing. It seems like it was all in vain.' The wound still festers.

She explains that as a Meira Paibi she is part of civil society and stands in solidarity with other people in their protest against the savage rape and killing of Manorama. Thus, 14 July was the day when a group of women rose and came together. 'Like the Nupi Lan, women rise to protect the menfolk. It was a secret deal. Even the press was not invited in case the news was leaked and then the government would come to know. The women swore not to reveal details about the protest to anyone, not even to their family members,' she says.

They knew they had to perform this courageous task with impeccable teamwork and co-ordination. They had decided on a signal – one of the women would stretch her arms and pull off her enaphi. That would be the signal for all of them to come closer and strip.

She called up a studio owner to bring two or three reliable press people who would not leak the information. Exactly at 10 am, the women stripped and walked to the main gate. They started shaking the gate. 'The security guards with guns came rushing towards us but their officer stopped them. The officer came forward, folded his hands and asked us to stop the protest,' she recalls. The armymen could not touch the women as they were naked, and so they had to call in their women colleagues and it was when they came that a battle ensued between them and the Imas.

Ima Mema is fortunate that nobody in her immediate family has suffered because of AFSPA. But fear and anxiety have become a constant factor in their lives, and she is perturbed over the suffering of innocent people as a result of this prolonged conflict. She starts citing examples such as the one about the lady called Naobi, who had to spend ten days in the custody of the security forces. She was so disturbed by the incident that she is still unable to express what happened to her. It's been a year now and all that she has been able to scream out is, 'My life is useless now.' Similarly, Sanamacha, a Class X student was picked up by the army because his name was similar to that of a militant. It was clearly a case of mistaken identity. But he's been missing for the past ten years.

The Manorama incident was the turning point for Ima Mema. Along with the other Imas, she took the step of challenging the security forces and fighting to remove them from Kangla Fort. But when she looks back, she finds it hard to believe that she was involved in this singular event, which will be remembered by posterity. 'My family members found it hard to believe that I could do something like this. My grandchildren laughed at me and I laughed with them,' she smiles.

Ima Mema has had many sleepless nights. She is often troubled by thoughts of her community. Sitting on a low stool, she looks towards the Tulsi plant in the courtyard and folds her hands and offers a silent prayer. 'I pray to God to grant me a sound sleep. Even on the night prior to the protest I could sleep only in the morning. But I had a sound sleep after the protest was over,' she says.

In her humble surroundings, Ima Mema is remarkably resilient. She calls herself an ordinary woman who has managed to survive in Manipur and, according to her, she has no fear of death. 'When my mother died, I did cry for some time. Her memory is still alive in my mind but I survived. I felt the same when my husband died. He remains in our hearts as a faint memory but the rest of us survived.'

Her only wish now is to witness the repeal of the AFSPA before she dies. She wants her grandchildren to live in peace. As we talk, her daughter joins us. Ima Mema looks at her and says, 'She will carry on the battle. It's the least she can do for society. Even if she dies for this cause, it does not matter.'

5

Ima Lourembam Nganbi, aka Ima Nganbi:
The English-Speaking Mother

For Ima Nganbi, it's an annual ritual every year.

She is waiting. She has been waiting since 2000. Ima Nganbi sits on a concrete bench in front of the Special Isolation Ward of J. N. Hospital in Manipur's capital city Imphal. She is smiling, despite the bumpy ride she has taken in an autorickshaw traversing a long stretch of 28 kms from her hometown, Bishenpur, to Imphal. She mostly travels by bus. But this year she came in an auto rickshaw because of a nagging pain in her leg.

Also waiting inside the special ward in the hospital is the iconic Iron Lady of Manipur, Irom Sharmila. Force-fed through a nose pipe, she has been fasting since 4 November 2000 to protest against the imposition of the AFSPA in the state. Sharmila has been arrested according to Indian legal provisions (IPC Section 309) for attempted suicide that legally allows imprisonment for a maximum of one year at a time. And every year, almost like a big farce, Sharmila is ceremonially released on March 7 for a day or two and then rearrested as she refuses to break her fast.

Defying the constraints of age, fading eyesight and creaking bones, it's a date Ima Nganbi never misses. She will come and wait for Sharmila's ceremonial release. She waits to escort Sharmila out. In the midst of the growing crowd comprising of the resolute Imas and some local media persons, Ima Nganbi spots me and gestures at me to sit near her. I squeeze myself on the bench as she puts her arm around me. 'Like you, Sharmila is also my daughter. I have come to meet her,' she smiles as she clasps my hand. As edgy policemen guard the premises, many other Imas gather and wait anxiously – some squat on the ground, some stand, some chat with each other, some wait silently –all waiting for their 'daughter' to emerge from captivity towards an ephemeral freedom of one or two nights. Usually, I am in Imphal for my reporting assignments but this time I had come to attend the annual general meeting of the Network of Women in Media, of which I am a member.

The portly Ima adjusts her golden-rimmed spectacles and makes a call from her mobile phone. The phone hangs around her neck with a string. 'I keep losing my phone,' she explains. Her hair, tied neatly in a bun, is streaked with grey. In her ears she wears small earrings of gold which have white stones embedded in them. She holds on to the crutch in her hand, it's clear she's in great pain, she flinches from time to time as the pain hits her. She tells me that it was in December 2005 that she fell down and hurt her leg and since then, her mobility has been restricted and she has been confined to her home for three long years. As we both wait, I tell her how much I relish *iromba* (a traditional dish made of dried fish). Ima Nganbi says, 'Why don't you come home? I will cook for you.'

Just then, the collapsible gates of the isolation ward open and Sharmila emerges, almost like a princess in exile. She is ushered out by two nurses. Almost instinctively, the mothers take charge. They hold the frail Iron woman on both sides and slowly walk out to a makeshift tent at a distance where they will spend the limited nights of freedom with her. Sharmila is dressed in her traditional clothes and has on a pair of bathroom slippers. The enaphi covers her head and a light blanket with a floral print is wrapped around her to protect her from the cold. The feeding pipe stuck in Sharmila's nose is used to force-feed her and is like a festering open wound that hurts the Imas surrounding her. The makeshift tent is a venue for a relay hunger strike by the women – both young and old. They have also put up a huge poster of Sharmila in front of the tent and a banner says, 'Save Sharmila. Repeal AFSPA.'

Almost a year later when I visited Manipur again, I called Ima Nganbi and told her that I wanted to come and meet her. Ima insisted that I come and spend some time with her. The stretch from Imphal to Bishenpur, her hometown is verdant, with the road dotted with green fields and hills. I try to soak up the idyllic surroundings. I wish I could hop on to a bicycle and pedal my way through the countryside! Trees dot the landscape, interrupting lush fields of green crops. The farmers are seen reaping in the fields and young Meitei women in traditional phanek and enaphi with their colourful helmets occasionally speed past on their Kinetic Hondas.

Bishenpur is a quaint and lazy pocket town, quite neat compared to Imphal. On the face of it, it looks quite serene and peaceful, unlike the horror stories one gets to hear of in Imphal. Locating Ima Nganbi's house is not difficult as she is a popular figure in her hometown. A grocer gives me directions and I easily find my way.

Her house is neat. As in every Meitei household, there is a small temple and a tulsi plant in the courtyard. A tiny pond at the entrance of the house has more than six goldfish in it. Feeding the goldfish is her younger daughter Liana Limparani's favourite pastime. Ima remembers buying the goldfish with their metallic-sheen red, gold, white and silver bodies from a government fishery pond in Imphal. Once they'd bought them, the family were inspired to create their own miniature version of a similar pond they'd seen in the palace of the King of Manipur in Shillong in the Northeastern state of Meghalaya.

I think of the Manipuri king's palace in Shillong and am reminded of a poignant love story from the Bengali book *Annya ek Bir Bikram* (*The Other Bir Bikram*) by Pannalal Roy, a historian based in Agartala, the capital of Tripura. Bir Bikram Kishore Manikya, the king of Tripura, was denied the hand of his beloved, the Manipuri princess Anandi Devi. 'In 1937, King Bir Bikram had fallen in love with Anandi Devi while staying in the Tripura palace at Shillong, where the Manipuri royal family also had a palace,' Roy explained. The king was not allowed to marry the woman he loved because he had committed the sin of crossing the seven seas – considered polluting at the time. Anandi Devi died of a broken heart after her family turned down the king's proposal.

'I learnt about this incident from Manipuri poet L. Birmangal Singh, who heard it from octogenarian Binodini Devi, Maharaja Churachand Singh's daughter and sister of Anandi Devi. The princess's father, King Churachand Singh of Manipur, was favourably disposed towards the proposal. But royal priests and scholars convinced the king that the Tripura monarch had lost his faith and purity as he frequently crossed the 'black waters' and stayed in Europe and America. Heartbroken at the proposal being rejected, the princess fell sick and soon passed away.'[1]

Ima Nganbi has meanwhile gone in for a bath and she now emerges, looking fresh and relaxed. She welcomes me with an embrace and speaks to me in English. 'Please come in.' She is a science graduate from Imphal College and people still remember her as one of the most vocal protestors in front of the Kangla fort who screamed in English, 'We are the mothers of Manorama. Come and rape us.'

The verandah has been converted into a sparse living room with a wooden sofa and a television perched on a table in one corner. The open verandah has been closed with a half wall of bamboo and the upper half has been covered with net. Light blue curtains with floral designs have been neatly hung in the portion covered by net. A table fan whirls in a corner of the room. Strikingly, a photo of Arambam Samarendra, founder of the outlawed insurgent group United National Liberation Front (UNLF) hangs in one corner. Formed on 24 November 1964, the UNLF is the oldest insurgent group in Manipur; their aim is independence and a socialist society. Samarendra had an impressive academic record – a post-graduate in military science from Pune University, he came overground in 1974 after the Manipur People's Party government headed by R. K. Dorendra Singh announced 'general amnesty'. He was also honoured with the Sahitya Akademi award. In June 2000, Samarendra was assassinated.

Ima Nganbi lays a *kauna* (water reed) mat on the floor and makes herself comfortable. Not secretive about her reverence for Samarendra, she searches for the right words as she explains, 'He wrote plays, songs and books which the people of Manipur should know. I have read two of his books. The fortitude and indomitability of Manipuri women have always been the focus of his plays.'

Nganbi's day starts very early, though she cannot move around much because of the pain in her leg. Her social activism keeps her busy. When she is not occupied with activism, she is hooked to television – watching mostly Hindu devotional programmes, animation versions of mythological shows like *Hanuman*, *Sri Krishna* and *Chhota Bheem*. She is not fond of films though. 'I know what's happening around the world as I watch news. I like cricket and know the words *chakka* (six) and *chauka* (four),' she says. She has no favourite cricketer but has heard of Sachin Tendulkar. She is also proud of boxing stars like Mary Kom and Monica Devi from her state.

She is also the popular storyteller of the neighbour-hood. Children in her locality love being with her, and listen to an exhaustive and absorbing carnival of stories of kings, queens, battlefields, fairies, giants and witches. She tells me that she is an unlucky woman as she has never seen her grandparents. 'There was nobody to tell me good stories,' she rues.

As we sit talking, she glances at the copy of *Tehelka* magazine I have with me that features the LTTE supremo Prabhakaran on the cover. She picks it up, scans it and says, 'I have a feeling that like a phoenix, Prabhakaran will rise again.' She admits that she does not know much about the LTTE or Prabhakaran. But she feels that the demands of the underground groups of Manipur are justified as they are fighting for the freedom of Manipur. Before merging with India, there was a merger agreement but the Government of India never heeded its provisions. 'Our groups are fighting for the freedom of Manipur,' she says.

Ima Nganbi has clearly always been a rebel. At the heart of her rebelliousness is a deep and poignant awareness of injustice. Born in 1950, she feels that she has survived in a world full of guns, bombs and grenades. Her encounters with security men have always been harsh. 'The security men want to kill, destroy and crush the UGs (underground groups). We say catch them and send them to jail. Don't kill them. Let the law take its course. And don't rape your mothers and sisters,' she argues.

In her life, she's had to face considerable hardship. Her father died early. Her mother, who never went to school, used to sell vegetables in Bishnupur bazaar to make both ends meet. But there have been happy moments too. Her life took a positive turn after she fell in love and got married to Kamal Louremba, her husband, who passed away in 1997. They belonged to neighbouring localities and their love blossomed when he went to take his class X board exam at the exam centre in Moirang. Her sister was also studying there and Nganbi used to go and meet her. She proudly talks about her husband as the first man who graduated with honours in Pharmaceuticals (B Pharm) in Manipur. He set up a dispensary in Loktak. He also worked as a demonstrator of Pharmacology at the Regional Institute of Medical Sciences (RIMS), Imphal. Later, he resigned and resorted to activism and became the founder secretary of the Workers Union, Loktak project. Her activism started when she joined the Nishabandh (campaign against alcoholism) movement. She tells me, My husband used to drink but never fought with me.'

She has two sons and two daughters. Her eldest daughter, Linthoi Nganbi is a postgraduate and works as a lecturer in a private college. Her other children are still studying. She wants her daughter to study further but is also looking for a groom. Like all mothers, she too has aspirations for a 'good' son-in-law. She smiles, 'He should be handsome and educated. He should also have a decent job.'

Ima makes me feel so much at home that I have no inhibitions in asking if I can stay on and have lunch with her. Her daughters are already in the kitchen preparing mouth-watering *iromba*, chicken curry and rice. As they lay the mat to serve me, a group of kids from the neighbourhood come for tuitions with her daughter. Her daughter tells them, 'We have a guest now. Come at 4 pm.' The kids peer at me and go away, talking among themselves.

I settle down and start chatting with Ima. She tells me how a brush with security forces is an everyday grim reality in Manipur. Once her eldest son was picked up by commandos at the police station. Some women came running and told her. 'I went to the police station and told them that he is my son. They released him after some questioning,' she says. Once she and her daughter were arrested under the National Security Act, 1980 which allows for preventive detention, and were jailed for two and a half months. They were protesting the death of a 32-year-old man called Pebam Chittaranjan, a young activist of the Manipuri Students' Federation, who took the extreme step of self-immolation at Bishnupur Bazar in Imphal to protest against the government's failure to repeal the repressive AFSPA.

The security men at every street corner have never asked her for an identity card, though they stop her for frisking. She smiles and asks them to go ahead and do their duty. Most often they say, 'Maaji (mother), please walk through.' For her, Independence Day every year is a day when life freezes in Manipur. 'It is celebrated by politicians under the shadow of guns and boycott calls by the militant groups,' she points out.

She remembers celebrating Independence Day as a child in school though – when she was inspired by the stories of Mahatma Gandhi and Jawaharlal Nehru. 'I cried a lot when Indira Gandhi was assassinated,' she says. She finds India's national anthem very thoughtful, and tells me that she used to respect it and stand up whenever it was sung. 'But I don't want to sing it anymore or stand up when it is played,' she says.

She has a rather acerbic take on contemporary life in Manipur. For Nganbi and her associates, there is a date in the calendar that is particularly significant: 15 October, the day Manipur became a part of India by signing the merger agreement. Manipur was earlier a princely state under British rule. The Maharaja of Manipur was coerced to sign the Instrument of Accession on 11 August 1947. After this, Defence, Communication and External Affairs came under the exclusive jurisdiction of New Delhi. Thereafter, Manipur became a part of the Indian Union.[2]

Instead of celebrating Independence Day on 15 August, Ima Nganbi and her friends burn copies of the Manipur merger agreement on 15 October every year and scream slogans like 'Loilam leingak muthatsi' (We want freedom), 'Ning tamna hinghallu' (Down with Indian Rule). 'We do not feel that we are independent in the midst of a draconian Act like AFSPA. We feel like we are servants of the Indian government,' she says.

Much to the consternation of the security forces, these indignant older women also stage protests on 26 January (Republic Day) every year. On these two days, the police keep a watch on them. But every time, they outwit the security forces. They plan well ahead and go to some remote village where the security forces cannot trace them. They hold meetings where they talk about their origins. 'Indian democracy is not a democracy. It's more like a military rule,' she says, fiddling with the four lucky stones she wears on her fingers to protect herself from the evil eye.

The Manorama incident provoked many bottled-up emotions. Nganbi recalls it as repugnant. The security forces had vilified and raped so many women before – either openly or secretly. It was getting intolerable for the people of Manipur, especially women. She had seen pictures of Manorama's defaced body and read about her mutilated private parts in the newspapers.

When she was invited for the all-important meeting at the Macha Leima office on 14 July, curfew had been imposed in Imphal and there were no buses plying. She coaxed an auto-driver to take her to Imphal. The auto-driver charged an exorbitant sum of a thousand rupees though it usually only takes around Rs 400 for the 28 km stretch from Bishenpur to Imphal. But the determined woman was ready to fish out the amount as, no matter what, she had to reach Imphal. She could not afford to miss the meeting. After getting down from the auto-rickshaw, she slowly trudged to the Macha Leima office, but the meeting was almost over by then and many women had left. She was startled when she came to know of the decision the mothers had taken. She thought about it for a while as she sipped some water, and then she said she too would like to join in. But she knew also that if she had to participate in the protest the next morning, she had to stay back in Imphal that night. It was difficult to go back home and come back again early the next morning. So she decided to stay back in another protestor, Tombi's house. 'My family members are used to my absences from home. They do not worry when I do not return for two or three days,' she smiles.

It was long night. There was a feeling of both restlessness and apprehension. Many felt a sense of impending doom, as if anything could happen at any moment. Lying on the bed next to Tombi, she had a long discussion with her. Tombi, 46, agreed to participate but only to collect their clothes. But Ima Nganbi tried to persuade her to join in the act of stripping as well. They talked for three long hours – from 7 pm to 10 pm. Nganbi finally managed to convince Tombi that it was her duty too, to protect their dignity of women and to fight for the truth. Tombi agreed and then, exhausted, she dozed off. Nganbi slept only for half an hour that night and woke up early. She brushed her teeth, had a cup of tea and some biscuits. Both of them took an auto rickshaw and went to the Macha Leima office.

With a silent prayer in their hearts, they geared up for the protest and took off their inner clothes and jewellery. Ima was anxious and also felt a strange sort of numbness. She was murmuring a prayer and hoping that the protest would be successful. A few of them were shaky. One was constantly biting her nails. Nganbi gave them a little talking to, saying they should not be anxious as they were simply doing their duty.

Then the moment was there and they got into two vans. A few women came from the Macha Leima office to Kangla which is located at a distance of 3 kilometres. They reached Kangla at around 9 am and stood separately in different places, so that nobody would suspect anything. There could be no false starts.

They assembled near the Kangla gate and the security guards thought that they were coming to see the Kangla Fort. Nganbi had the two banners held securely under her enaphi. They were somewhat fearful of what lay ahead; no one had really wanted to carry the banners, but she now had them. When they neared the gate, the guard, who was a Meitei man, asked them to stop, saying, 'Wait, wait.' As one of the Imas gave the agreed signal, they began to strip and unfurled the banner.

While the protest was on, she could see the Commanding Officer (CO) of Assam Rifles. He came forward and bowed before the nude mothers with a Namaste and went back. All the soldiers were completely dumbstruck. When some of the security guards warned them to leave, the mothers yelled at them, 'You are also Manipuri. Don't you know what the army is doing? Why are you threatening us? We want to beat you, come here. You are a mere servant of the security forces.'

The livid mothers started banging at the gates of the Kangla fort. The security guards ran towards them. Then the women cautioned them, throwing patriarchy back at them. 'Don't come near us. Don't you dare touch us. If this phanek touches any man, he will be accursed all his life and will be under the control of the women.' The armed men were afraid to come forward.

The phanek, Ima Nganbi tells me, is not a garment to be trifled with in Meitei society. 'According to ancient lore, if a man wears a dress made from the used phanek (women's skirt, belonging to the Meitei mothers and grandmothers), it ushers in prosperity. It also leads to victories in hunting expeditions and battles. There is a conviction that amulets made from a piece of a mother's phanek can protect one from the evil eye.' It is said that Manipur's freedom fighter Paona Brajabashi put a piece of his mother's phanek in an amulet. Only when he removed it did he die.

Elders do not touch a phanek as a mark of respect. The women screamed at the soldiers, 'If you touch our phanek, we will beat you with it instead of a stick. We will challenge your guns with a phanek.' And every Meitei man knows what this can mean.

As the women screamed and protested for nearly an hour, the security forces stood stunned and helpless in front of the incensed mothers. After a while, the women's helpers picked up their phaneks and gave them back to the women who put them on again. With the phanek, Ima said she seemed to come back to normal life. By this time some of the women had fainted and had to be taken to the nearby J.N. hospital. Nganbi was asked by the policewomen to get into the police jeep, but she refused. She trudged her way to the office of Macha Leima. 'I felt so drained. And I could feel a sense of shame and I fainted.'

The nude protest led to chaos. Immediately, curfew was announced and schools, colleges and offices shut down and people ran for their lives. Ima Nganbi knew that she had to return home that day, no matter how she did it. She walked from the Macha Leima office to the bus junction at Keisamphat at around 2 pm. She boarded a bus. After all that anxiety, now that the deed had been done, she felt like she was floating on air. She looked around the bus, wondering if any of the passengers had seen her protesting. Nobody asked her anything and she consoled herself that nobody had seen her. Somehow she had to reach home.

On their arrival at the bus stand, she met a friend who insisted they go to a wayside eatery for tea and snacks at Bishenpur Bazar. It was nearly 4 in the evening and she was weary and hungry so she agreed. When they found a small eatery, a young boy looked at her and said, laughingly, 'The Meira Paibis are really robust and healthy.' And then, he suddenly looked at her more carefully and said, 'Aren't you the protestor who screamed in English? I saw you on the local channel at 3 pm today.'

Nganbi was at a loss for words. Almost spontaneously,

she started denying that she'd been in Imphal for the protest. But the boy laughed and said, 'I know you can speak in English.' Nganbi was relieved that her friend sitting with her did not understand anything.

She asked her friend to hurry up and walked home with her. She closed the door behind her, hoping nobody had seen her. Just then some children came for tuitions and they were chattering, 'Grandmother spoke in English at the Kangla.' Her children got to know and asked her if what they were hearing was true. She then told them everything. Gradually, when it got dark, the shame started to set in and she became quite flustered. But she tried not to think. The television channels had been blacked out by 3 pm, so not many people knew about the protest. She went off to sleep and, exhausted, slept soundly.

Early in the morning when the raucous calls of the crows rang out in the locality, she continued to lie in bed, her eyes shut, praying that morning would never come and she would not have to face the world. When the newspaper man brought the paper, her son quickly picked it up and hid it. The mothers' protest had hit the local headlines. There was no hiding things any more. Curious neighbours and other Meira Paibis came and asked her for details. Ima Nganbi told me, 'It's still all a blur in my head. For a few days, I did not go anywhere. Not many came to meet me either.' She did not look at the newspapers herself as she felt she had done what she had to do. 'I did not feel the need to see the newspaper,' she says.

In her heart she still carries the same dreams: the repeal of AFSPA and Irom Sharmila's return to a normal life [this latter has since happened. Sharmila gave up her fast in 2016]. She speaks of the moment of protest with pride, and with anger at some of the reactions the Imas got. 'We did it for the people of Manipur,' she says, 'we are not prostitutes.' The scene at the Kangla fort haunts her, she comes from a very conservative community and it took considerable courage to do what she and her companions did that day. I tell her this and thank her for her courage as I leave.

6

Loitam Ibetombi (1948–2013), aka Ima Ibetombi: Heroism Offstage

The microphone squawks as the announcer speaks about the play, the workshop and the richness of Manipuri theatre. Ever since I read about Heisnam Kanhailal and his wife Sabitri's experiments with theatre, I have wanted to meet this interesting couple. In the year 2003, when I heard that Kanhailal was in town, I went to meet him at the guest house of Srimanta Sankardev Kalakshetra, Guwahati's cultural hub.

I wait for him. I see him instructing a group of young actors. He comes and sits next to me and smiles. It's nearing lunchtime. 'You know, I love Assamese cuisine. We're from the same rice culture, we possess the same temperament.' He smiles as he relaxes into the sofa. He loves his interludes in Guwahati city, the gateway to Northeast India. He looks at the sunny lawn outside and, in his sonorous voice, says, 'Guwahati is like my second home.'

Heisnam Kanhailal likes working with young artistes. In Guwahati too, he has been conducting a theatre workshop. Set up in 1969, Kanhailal's theatre group, Kalakshetra Manipur, experiments with alternative theatre. In 1985, he became the first person from Northeast India to have received the Sangeet Natak Akademi award in the field of modern theatre. He was awarded the Padmashri in 2004.

While talking to him, I had no inkling that he and his wife Sabitri would shake up the world of theatre with their bold experiment just a year later. For this theatre couple from Manipur, the year 2000 was almost like a culmination of a lifelong engagement – both philosophically and in the sense of commitment – with conflict, violence, molestation, death.

Ironically, it was four years before the historic nude protest at Kangla that Heisnam Kanhailal and his wife Heisnam Sabitri tried a bold experiment with Mahasweta Devi's play 'Draupadi'. Sabitri appeared nude on stage: in a dramatic moment, in confrontation with the army, she throws off her clothes and dares the solder to look at her body. Like the soldiers at Kangla, the ones in the play are shamed at this exposure of the female body. Four years later, in 2004, when a group of Manipuri women walked on the streets of Imphal to the Assam Rifles headquarters and disrobed to protest, it was as if 'Draupadi' had come alive again.

As I try to trace similarities between the Kangla nude protest and Sabitri and Kanhailal's bold experiment with 'Draupadi', the veteran theatre person remarks, 'What is common between the incident and the play is that they both portray the decades-long oppression by security forces in the region.' Their play triggered no small tremors in their home state, raising a new level of engagement with the chronic problems plaguing Manipur.

When the nude protest took place at Kangla in 2004, the couple was in Delhi. They were conducting theatre classes there. A friend informed them about the protest. Sabitri was in tears when she heard the news. 'I was also told that the following day local newspapers carried headlines of the protest that the play was 're-enacted' at Kangla,' says Kanhailal. Some even started calling him 'chingu', a Meitei word meaning a man who can predict the future.

Deeply committed and convinced by their own belief, this charismatic couple used theatrical techniques to portray the nakedness in their initial production of 'Draupadi'. For Sabitri, there was a lingering desire to perform the act of nakedness in its truest sense. Therefore, when they were about to stage the play at the National School of Drama (NSD), New Delhi in March

2000, Heisnam conceded to his artiste wife's request. 'All this while, Sabitri was not satisfied with her performance. She wanted to perform the act of nakedness in its truest sense. I, as a director gave instant approval to her proposal. But we were aware of the possible hurdles that we would face,' he says.

Sabitri's first nude appearance was at NSD Delhi. It was a disquieting experience for the audience. 'I remember Sonal Mansingh came to the green room after the play. She was in tears,' says Kanhailal.

Though I had not seen the play myself but I had read a poignant piece by Trina Nileena Banerjee, who wrote after watching the play, 'At the time that I watched this performance, I was in college. Sabitri Heisnam would then have been in her early-60s. I remember clearly that some women in the audience walked out in the middle of this scene. Some sobbed. Some wept loudly outside the hall after it was over. Most men were frozen into a stunned, dazed kind of silence. Theatrical conventions had been broken. But, something bigger than that had happened simultaneously. A naked woman's body had refused to titillate, to evoke lust or desire, to assume forms that were publicly considered immoral – but were implicitly more acceptable than this powerful, horrifying, completely autonomous nakedness.'[3]

Their next show was in Imphal, the same year, in the month of April. The show was part of a theatre festival. After the show, there was a heated debate. In conservative Meitei society, Sabitri's act met with severe criticism from many quarters. Many wrote against the play. It became a subject of debate among writers, social commentators and the local media.

The couple decided not to give any sort of feedback or reaction to the criticism at that point of time. The play was more like a catharsis for the theatre couple. Heisnam explained that it was important to put the socio-political landscape of Northeast India, and Manipur in particular, in perspective. For the last three decades, they'd been hearing about atrocities committed against women by the security forces. He felt that it was disheartening to hear about such atrocities. In most cases, the victims tended to suppress their feelings out of fear and shame, they assumed that they had been disgraced. 'I believe this mindset among the women has been influenced by the socio-cultural practices and conditioning,' said Kanhailal.

One particular incident perturbed them both. In 1996, a woman called Ahanjaobi who was raped by the security forces during a search operation inside her house, came out in public to speak about the rape. It was a shocking revelation. Her courage gave the couple the strength and inspiration to do something about these issues.

Meanwhile, their friend, Samik Bandyopadhay, a Kolkata-based theatre critic, mentioned Mahasweta Devi's short story 'Draupadi' during their conversations. In 1999, the couple went to Mumbai to visit Madhushree

Dutta, executive director of Majlis, a centre for rights discourse and multi-disciplinary art initiatives in Mumbai. Madhushree was working on a film and Sabitri was one of the actors. Kanhailal somehow stumbled on Mahasweta's 'Draupadi' on the bookshelves at the Majlis office. The story instantly moved him and he decided to enact the play on stage. It was in January 2000 that Kalakshetra completed rehearsal of the play.

They mesmerized and provoked the audience by staging the play in different parts of India. They have staged more than a dozen shows in Kolkata alone. After each show, the reaction has been similar to what happened in Delhi when Sabitri first appeared naked on stage. The play was also staged at the Dhaka International Festival. Then it was shown in Agartala, Tripura as well as elsewhere. 'We saw that the audiences were spellbound after every show of 'Draupadi'. We are glad that the play was staged in Imphal in 2014 during the International Theatre Exposition, held in collaboration with Manipur University. The international delegates as well as the audience of Imphal received the play with great appreciation,' he said.

The opulent tapestry of theatre that exists in the bullet-ridden social fabric of Manipur is very interesting. Explaining the rich cultural heritage of Manipur, an activist friend once told me, 'In Manipur, guns and roses exist together.' And, when I meet the charming Loitam Ibetombi, I know she is an actor.

With a combination of poise, grace and beauty on the one hand and a fiery spirit on the other, she tries to reclaim her past as she shows me her beautiful black and white photograph which she uses as a screen saver on her mobile phone. She is svelte and exquisitely beautiful, like the dream-like film stars of yesteryear.

As I sit with her on the verandah of the house, she begins to tell me about her life which seems to sprawl across a crowded canvas. I gather that her past life is packed with action. She smiles as she talks about her professional life as an actor. As part of the Manipur Dramatic Union (MDU) – the oldest theatre group in Manipur that was set up in 1931 – she went to Allahabad for a drama competition, and there, was given the all-India best actress award. Coping with her father's resistance to her being an actor was not easy. But people persuaded him to allow her to act. She once also acted in a Meitei film. 'I was even contemplating a career in Bollywood. I wanted to be like Madhubala,' she bursts out laughing.

Remembering the Manipur of her younger days, she laughs, a laugh that lights up her beautiful face. 'The times were different when I was young. The only scary thing was the young goons in the neighbourhood waiting to woo me.' But then her sister was a policewoman, so these goons were easily frightened off. Her sister, Loitam Bino was another spunky woman. She was the first woman to join the police force in Manipur. The women's police force was established in 1961 with the selection of Loitam Bino as Head Constable and six others as constables.[4] Ibetombi laughs as she narrates this anecdote, 'After my sister joined the police, I was protesting on the road and was burning a tyre. My sister came, hit me and then arrested me.'

Ima Ibetombi has many sides to her personality. She is also known for her dulcet voice and has been a graded radio artiste with All India Radio (AIR). But she stopped singing after her husband's death – he used to work for the SSB (*Sashastra Seema Bal*) as a stenographer. Speaking of his death, the laughter dies and the tears begin to fall. I try to console her. She wipes her tears with her enaphi and says, 'I could not take care of my only son when he died of jaundice in 2000. I was busy with my social activism. I still have guilt about that.' The atmosphere becomes sombre as Ibetombi begins to talk about the sad chapters of her life, as one tragedy seemed to follow another. She had barely recovered from her son's death when, six months later, during the 18 June uprising in 2001, her husband suffered a stroke and died. At this time too, she was busy being an activist. 'One activist was hit by a bullet and my husband thought it was I who was hit. He was so worried that his blood pressure shot up and he and died of a stroke,' she says.

We're in a room with faded yellow walls, talking. Her niece brings us coffee. She clutches the glass as if looking for support in the hot coffee. Her greatest remorse is that she could not even take part in her husband's funeral rites as she was running away from the police. They were keeping a constant vigil at her house. She could not afford to be seen there as the arrest warrant said she could be picked up only from her house. She could come home only on the day of the *shraddha*, the funeral rites. But that too was a brief visit. While she was there, suddenly, jeeploads of police came to arrest her; she managed to flee though the back door.

The news of Manorama's killing was very upsetting for Ibetombi. She and some friends went to have a look at Manorama's body in the morgue. 'It was a spine-chilling experience. I felt that if they were not stopped, such grisly killings might reach every door,' she says. The incident seemed ominous, almost a precursor of things to come. It seemed like a do-or-die situation.

She tries to string together memories of her family's past. She draws inspiration from her illustrious grandparents. Her grandmother, Tombi Macha, who was later conferred the title Loudroubi, was a legendary leader of the Nupi Lan movement. Ibetombi was not born then. She heard stories of her famous grandmother's valour from her father. 'She taught me so much. She taught me how it is important to follow your heart and to do what you wish to do,' she says with a sense of pride.

And her grandfather went to Germany to fight in World War II. He got a gallantry award from the British. She asks me to wait as she opens her almirah to show us the medals wrapped carefully in three layers, a piece of cloth, then polythene and then paper.

I listen as Ibetombi animatedly tells me all the things that she wanted to be and all the things she wanted to do. I can see her as a child as she talks about her happy and secure childhood. It was fun growing up with ten siblings – six sisters and four brothers – she says. She loved to sing and won a gold medal for her singing. Though she studied only till class X, she played hockey, javelin, shot put, badminton.

Her father was a politician but he never contested elections. He was editor of a newspaper called 'Praja' (meaning public). However, politics is of no interest to her. 'I don't want to be a politician. I had once gone out to vote but did not vote because the queue was very long,' she says, almost bored at the prospect.

Just then two young boys come to meet her. They are about to leave. She kisses them on their foreheads. She now lives with her sister and sister-in-law. The death of her son and husband left a void in her heart. 'I am very lonely now. But I have also mellowed and become more accepting now,' she sighs.

The reality of life in Manipur perturbs her. She is pained by the law and order situation which has now gone from bad to worse. After the Manorama incident, Ibetombi had a fear that other girls might meet with the same fate. Therefore, she formed a women's committee. 'When the Kangla protest happened, very few had mobile phones. There was curfew and people could travel only by walking from one place to the other. It was a decision of around 150 women but only 12 of them turned up,' she says.

She is not very hopeful of change – she's deeply dissatisfied with the central government's apathy to Sharmila's protest. She is not interested in the issues raised by the underground groups. But one thing that troubles her is the future of the young who have grown up with violence and conflict. She tells me, 'The mothers have a big role to play as they give birth. As a mother, it is difficult to answer the contradictions in Manipuri society which produces ace sportspersons as well as theatre artistes.'

Meitei women are unique as they are deeply concerned about the society they live in and they are involved in various social organizations. Ima Ibetombi is not an exception. She is also the president of Sangaipat women Development-cum-Marketing Association, an NGO. She wants everyone to come together. However, she is also cynical of opportunists. 'Some Imas turned up only to hog the limelight,' she says.

The nude protest was not really a difficult decision, according to her, it was an all-stakes-in situation. She did not inform her family members that she was going to take part in it. The women knew that they were going to challenge someone with guns. So they were ready to get killed. The policemen too cried with them. She sounds angry as she recalls the moment, 'If the police came forward we would have torn their clothes off. We were like goddess Kali – ready to devour.' After the protest, she fell unconscious because her blood pressure was quite low. Her granddaughters were angry with her. She told them, 'You are not the only granddaughters for me, all the young girls are my granddaughters.' She became a heroine overnight. Her neighbours showed a lot of solidarity. However, she is not in touch with Manorama's family.

She is proud of what they did that day. But, the actress in her speaks out. I am amused as she says, 'I had the longest hair. Even in the video footage you can see it.' When I had met Ibetombi, she was under medical supervision as three of her vertebrae were displaced when a security man had hit her with the butt of his gun. She showed me rubber bullet shot wounds. 'I don't think I will survive another ten years. But after I die, I would like to be remembered like my illustrious grandmother,' she says.

As I move away I see a framed photograph on the fading wall with these words inscribed in it, 'Perhaps one day we can all walk tall – our minds without fear, and our heads held high, in a world free of narrow domestic walls.'

(Loitam Ibetombi died in 2013.)

7

Haobam Ongbi Tombi Devi, aka Ima Tombi: The Youngest of Them All

A friend tells me a hilarious 'pumpkin story'. Pumpkins from Myanmar are very popular in Manipur. When Indian pumpkins don't sell too well, traders secretly take them on a truck to the Myanmar border. From there they come back with the same truckloads of pumpkins. People think they are Myanmarese pumpkins, and then they sell like hot cakes! Most of these pumpkins and other goods from Myanmar like smoked and dry fish, vegetables, electronic goods and even drugs are sold in Singjamei, a bustling market in Imphal East district, which connects India to Myanmar. This market is located on the Indo-Myanmar high road that leads to Moreh, the border town with the neighbouring country. The area also has a considerable number of drug addicts as it is also one of the main drug routes.

One fine afternoon, it is business as usual at a well-stacked pharmacy at Singjamei, when an 11-year-old girl steps into a pharmacy and asks for a packet of sanitary pads. As is the usual practice, the shopkeeper hastily tries to wrap it in a piece of newspaper. He is taken aback when she stops him. Amused at the shopkeeper's consternation, she tells him, 'There is nothing shameful about sanitary pads. I would like to carry the packet without concealing it in a piece of newspaper.' A few people standing in the shop glare at her. An amused woman standing in the shop smiles at her. She walks off confidently from the shop. This plucky girl is Tamanna, daughter of health activist Chanam Urmila.

The quickest way to introduce 36-year-old Urmila is as a 'woman on a red mission'. She is trying to bust myths and taboos around menstruation and the reproductive health of women. She has also been educating Tamanna about this, and as a learning exercise, she asked her daughter to go buy a packet of sanitary pads. Her idea was to make her shed all inhibitions about menstruation or sanitary pads. 'I explained to her that it is a normal and healthy phenomenon. We have to understand that menstrual blood is not impure. It's after all a mind game. Little do they know that the shame will act as the biggest obstacle in making good health choices,' says Urmila.

Every year, she hosts a 'red' journey on the occasion of International Menstrual Hygiene Day from 29 March to 28 May. She urges all girls to wear red through these two months every day and convey the message 'We are girls and we menstruate.' They can wear anything that is red – tops, shirts, necklaces, hair clips, earrings, bracelets, badges, scarves, flip flops and sandals, even bags and pouches. People can also 'share' the campaign album, pictures, status updates or posts with friends on social media. The idea is to initiate a dialogue, end the shame and bring in pride.

Based in Bangalore, Urmila was described by a newspaper as the 'Manipuri woman who busts myths around menstruation'. A post-graduate in Anthropology, Urmila started off as a journalist writing about the lives of women and especially about their health and the taboos associated with a woman's monthly cycle. She also wrote for various media houses.

As an army officer's daughter, she has lived all over India. She has a wealth of information on cultural taboos that impact women. She wanted to do something more than just write about this so she came up with the idea to start a campaign called Breaking the Silence, with the tagline, 'Let's celebrate the red droplets' on social media. Undaunted by the paucity of resources, Urmila's most important tool was her smartphone.

When Urmila flagged off her campaign, she did not realize that it would be so popular. She was excited when WASH United, an NGO that works on sanitation and health, listed her campaign in their calendar as a not-to-be-missed event. It was the only campaign being run by an individual from within her home. One thing led to another. She won the National Laadli Media and Advertising Award for Gender Sensitivity in 2015 when her global campaign 'Breaking the Silence' was adjudged the most powerful campaign in the country for using technology, innovation and social media to question traditional norms that are crippling for girls and women. As she travels all over Manipur for her campaign, she says she can see no discourse on the reproductive health of adolescent girls and women.

She is now involved in a number of activities in Manipur, focusing on the following districts: Ukhrul, Tamenglong, Churachandpur, Senapati and Chandel. 'In Meitei society, women are not supposed to cook, go to the temple or even talk about '*thagi khongchat*' (the Meitei term for menstruation). It's a norm in Manipur for women to tear and use a part of their mother's phanek during their periods. I used to use the phanek, which is coarse, hard fabric, usually of polyester. It is definitely not the best fabric to be used for sanitary material. There are girls who are into outdoor activities, gradually they become introverts,' she says. She recalls how in Uganda, women are so poor that they use polythene, tissues or sand wrapped in cotton cloth, to check the blood flow. 'We went there to teach them to make their own sanitary pads,' she says.

Urmila is appalled that Meitei women never questioned these taboos and unhygienic practices. They run marketplaces and are involved in many outdoor activities. 'But when it comes to her own dignity, the woman is ignorant. She becomes an untouchable. They are also afraid of going to the doctor. There are many other myths and I am in the process of learning and understanding them,' she says. She is also trying to understand the problems of tribal women, mostly Christian. In Nepal, a woman is pushed out to a hut that is close to the place where the livestock is kept. Urmila asks, 'How can a woman feel empowered or have a sense of dignity when she is ostracized and secluded five days a month?'

Changing old rule books about traditional beliefs is not an easy task. She knows she is plugging new ideas to an unwilling audience. She is very discreet when she talks to a group of people. She starts off discussing ordinary everyday issues about life and gradually leads them to a discussion about menstrual hygiene.

She recalls holding a session with wives of Assam Rifles soldiers at the Family Welfare Centre of 40 Assam Rifles Keithekmanbi in Manipur. Most of these women stay at home because their husbands have transferable jobs. She spoke to them about the taboos associated with menstruation. 'My campaign focuses on reaching out to difficult-to-reach women and girls. And wives and daughters of soldiers are among these. We had a long discussion and most of the problems seem to be universal,' she says.

Her campaign is mostly through social media and

blogging for the urban population. But for rural areas, she adopts a novel strategy – night classes in the anganwadi centres, panchayat offices and government schools. She was also nominated for the global award '21 Leaders in the 21st Century Award 2015' that was held in Dallas, Texas in USA for her work on banishing taboos and myths around menstruation in communities and raising awareness on menstrual hygiene management. She is popularly known as 'Mama MHM' (menstrual hygiene management) by stakeholders in Uganda including the Network of Water and Sanitation (NETWAS-Uganda).

I think of Urmila's inspiring story, as I trudge the streets of Paona Bazar in Imphal looking for Ima Tombi, one of the gutsy women who took part in the historic nude protest, the youngest in the group. I asked my Meitei friend to describe Paona Bazar in one word. And she blurts out, 'Disarray'.

I am directed to a crammed lane in the heart of the busy Paona Bazar. It's like a labyrinth. It is difficult to believe that there can be so many small roadside eateries in this dark alley. One of them leads me up the poorly-lit steep stairs of an unventilated two-room space on the first floor. Ima Tombi's abode is in this tunnel-like passage along the main artery of Imphal's commercial hub. At the end of a grimy, dented street, a woman in her late forties sits on the floor and stares into nothingness. A group of children play in the slushy puddle nearby.

Ima Tombi is perched on a small stool in her cramped

eatery which resembles a shanty. My eyes are fixed on the wares she has on display. She sells rice and Ngangam – small fish fried with onion leaves and spices, a delicacy in Manipur. She makes up to Rs 700-800 a day. As I sit there, I have to adjust and more or less fold over to make room for the passers-by who try to make their way along the passage, hemmed in by similar pint-sized eateries. A slender moustached man appears and orders some Ngangam, which she wraps in a newspaper for him.

Her home is on the first floor of the ramshackle shop, up a wooden ladder. Her small abode has room even for her magnificent black dog, who she lovingly calls Macha ('child'). Macha barks at the passers-by and hops up and down the tapered staircase with Tombi's granddaughter. Tombi, a widow, stays with her only son and his family.

Petite and fair, Tombi doesn't look at all old, though she has four grandchildren. Macha is excited at the sight of newcomers and he paces up and down the staircase. Tombi asks her five-year-old granddaughter to keep him on a leash. Tombi's son works with a film producing company. She tells me, 'The Manipuri film industry has a huge market. These are films, mostly made in the VCD format and on a shoestring budget.'

After a ban imposed on Hindi films by the outlawed underground group Revolutionary Peoples Front (RPF) in September 2000, VCD films in Meitei have been flourishing. The RPF banned Hindi films and television shows as they believed they were 'corrupting Manipuri culture and language'. The movie theatres could not afford expensive Hollywood films and some of them screen out-dated films, months after they have been released worldwide. Many movie halls have closed down. Cable television stations also had to close because of the dearth of programmes. A couple of enterprising filmmakers looked at this as a god-sent opportunity and started churning out low-cost digital films in Meitei featuring home-grown actors.

Tombi tells me about the popularity of Korean films, drama and pop music. She points to some of the shops outside which have stacked DVDs. People seem to relish Korean films and dramas with sub-titles, possibly because of a similarity in looks, even body language, and food habits among both sets of people. A customer sitting in Ima Tombi's shop laughs, 'Some Korean films are so good that even Hollywood is copying them.'

However, diehard fans of Bollywood can still get access to the latest flicks through pirated dvds and satellite television channels. In fact, it was an emotional moment for many when the Priyanka Chopra starrer 'Mary Kom' was released in India. In Imphal too, huge hoardings and posters were put up in different locations but then it could not be screened anywhere since it was a Hindi film.

Local films in Meitei are screened in the cinema halls. Tombi does not much care for films even though Usha, a popular cinema hall, is right opposite her dark alley.

At any given time there are crowds of young men and women and children walking into or out of the hall. Waiting outside are people lining up for the next show of the latest Manipuri blockbuster as heavily armed commandos of the Manipur police eye them warily, sitting at streetcorners on their motorcycles.

Paona Bazar has two-storeyed buildings with shops on either side of the narrow road. One can come across all kinds of imported items like blankets, dresses, crockery, electronic items bought from Moreh, a town in Chandel district which is the Indo-Myanmar trading point. Ima Tombi tells me, 'Sitting here in Paona Bazar, I have witnessed many gory incidents of violence. Once, a man who had come for shopping with his infant son was killed by the commandos. This was in 2006. I was deeply pained by the sight.'

Originally from Wangkhei in Imphal East district, she settled here some 20 years ago, on property owned by her father-in-law, who had given a few shops on rent. Educated only up to Class I, Tombi was unaware of worldly matters for a long time. She was mainly concerned with the home, concentrating all her time and energy on household chores after her marriage at the age of 18. Terms like AFSPA were alien to her initially. 'Gradually, I got to know that AFSPA is a subversive law that has ruined our community. I am pained, though I have never suffered any personal loss. Life is a challenge in Manipur as killings take place almost every day,' she says.

Like many Manipuri women, she has always tried to keep herself busy doing things for society as a member of the Nupi Samaj, a women's organization. She helps whenever protest marches are to be organized. 'Since my childhood, I have seen my mother participate in Nishabandh, a movement against alcoholism. I used to follow the elderly women in that,' she says. And on the day of the iconic protest too, she followed in the footsteps of women older than her. Tombi, aged 49, was the youngest among the protestors. Interestingly, her name Tombi also literally means 'youngest of the siblings'.

Tombi was present at the meeting of the group of Meira Paibis when they took the decision to stage the nude protest. 'I was pained when I learnt how Manorama was killed and I was shocked when I saw her mutilated body. We had to do something so that the security forces would not dare to repeat the same act. We had to challenge them,' she says with a conviction that startles me. The women realized, she says, that all other forms of protest had been futile.

She had initially decided that she would join the protest but only to assist them. She would collect the clothes the protestors took off. 'But one of the elderly mothers convinced me that my role was equally important. At that time I did not realize the impact of the protest. I took some time to think over it. I felt that if these elderly women can make such a sacrifice, why not me? I was ready to die,' she says, admitting that it was a hard decision to make.

15 July 2004 was not a characteristic run-of-the-mill day for her. It was a day of reckoning. She was unusually quiet the day before. She woke up at the crack of dawn. She spoke about her last-minute epiphany, 'I avoided talking even to my grandchildren lest I blurt out something. I was tense. I remembered my vow not to tell anyone about our plans. We were afraid that someone might try to stop us,' she says.

This ordinary woman from such a humble background leaves me speechless as she speaks about the protest, 'Our decision was not to mock the women of Manipur. We did what was the need of the hour. I also felt a sense of shame when I stripped myself. But it was imperative. We had to do it. As our protest was so unique, other people in the world got to know of it. In future, people will remember it for this, its uniqueness,' she says.

This collective experience of stripping was cathartic for her. She was happy that she could do something for her people. 'I am ready to work for the repeal of the Act,' she says. She was happy that everyone, including her son, appreciated the step she took and she feels her life is richer now, Manipuri women are very strong, she says. 'I don't know if it's because of the bitter experience or if it is real courage, but we are very resilient. I feel proud that I am a woman and not a man.'

She tells me she has been to Delhi once to stage a

protest against the AFSPA. 'Delhi is so big. People in Delhi seemed so happy and safe,' a bewildered Tombi says with the innocence of a child. She was awestruck by the huge shops and the variety in the markets, but she did not get much time to look around. She joined in the protest against AFSPA at Jantar Mantar. On the day she was coming back, she bought herself a pair of shoes and toys for her granddaughter.

On her return from Delhi, her family and friends surrounded her and asked her hundreds of questions: Does Delhi look like Imphal? Was AFSPA enforced in Delhi too? Were people killed every day in Delhi like in Manipur? Did she see the house of the President of India? Or India Gate? Or Red Fort? I wonder at her innocence as she tells me, 'I know that the Prime Minister and the President of India stay in Delhi. We had, in fact gone to meet them but we could not. I am no longer interested to meet them. If I ever meet the Prime Minister, I will ask him to repeal AFSPA.'

Ima is happy to be in her birthplace in Manipur. 'I don't expect the comforts of Delhi here. But I want my people to be happy,' she says. Politicians do not inspire her. Nor does she have faith in them. Indeed, she did not even want to cast her vote in the elections. 'The elections are useless. It's a futile exercise. But since the candidate personally came begging for my vote, I went to cast my vote,' she says.

8

Chungkham Ongbi Jamini Devi, aka Ima Jamini: Just Like a Man

On the streets of Birmingham in the UK, a young Manipuri doctor Bishwajeet Elangbam's thoughts fly back and forth. The panorama of life and death plays out in his mind's eye. Working in Emergency Medicine in the West Midland Deanery, Bishwajeet glanced out of his hospital window one bright summer afternoon, and seemed to forget the odour of the antiseptic as he spotted the fragrant flowers in full bloom in the lawns outside. The sight momentarily transported him back to his homeland, where he grew up and did his schooling and his medical education from the Regional Institute of Medical Sciences (RIMS) at Imphal. He thought of the swaying bamboo groves around his house and the wild lilies in the pond in the backyard. Comparing it to the carefully cultivated flower patches in the picturesque landscape of England was an eye-opener in many ways.

He was charmed by the sense of belonging many British people had towards their own country. 'I believe this is the driving force for many of them. It helps them to turn the places they live into lively places one can take pride in,' he tells me.

As Bishwajeet explored more, he found that these beautiful gardens are a product of an initiative called 'Britain in Bloom Project' which works to brighten up neighbourhoods by involving the community. A horticultural campaign in the United Kingdom, it was initiated in 1963 by the British Tourist Board, and has been under the aegis of the Royal Horticultural Society (RHS) since 2002.

Bishwajeet started wondering if this could be replicated in the *leikais* of Manipur – he was sure it could revitalize the streets and public spaces of his conflict-ridden state. He says, 'This can re-energise and create a vital bond between the people and the land and hopefully nurture a sense of pride. That spirit is missing in Manipur and is possibly the reason for the severe deterioration and neglect of our land, slowly turning into areas of concrete slums and garbage-filled land. In short, the land is slowly losing its soul.' The idea lingered in his mind, and soon Bishwajeet started discussing it with his younger brother Satyajit Elangbam. 'We contemplated ways to tranform the historic Ima market in Imphal with beautiful flowers. It can add colour to the place and usher in a sense of pride and belonging among the people. Growing a few flowers doesn't cost much, but it connotes a thriving living spirit. A spirit that can bring a smile to anyone's face,' he points out.

The doctor's efforts bore fruit. 'Blooming Manipur' came into being and grew with the support of the European Manipuri Association (EMA), Manipur Housing and Urban Development of the Government of Manipur (MAHUD), Imphal Municipal Council and, importantly, the women leaders of the market. A community gardening project took off. He tried to rope in other Manipur related overseas organizations and people from Manipur living in Europe, who had seen how Britain in bloom was changing the streets and public places in UK.

One place followed another. Next in line was Moirang, a city and municipal council in Bishnupur district. Shortly after, some very kind people of Moirang started 'Blooming Moirang' by planting trees and flowers at their historic market. Around 200 Bauhinia trees were planted at a school at Thamnapokpi, Bishnupur district. This project was done independently. Bishwajeet and his team only guided them. Then, the European Manipuri Association in collaboration with the municipal councils of two district of Manipur, Thoubal and Kakching, planted flowers in their own local market areas.

Blooming Manipur has been creating a silent revolution in different parts of the state, even as the group has been looking at more innovative ideas, particularly using social media. The Facebook page of Blooming Manipur has been sending regular press releases and encouraging the concept of 'taking ownership and responsibility' of the place where they live. 'I hope that one day we will have streets, local markets, sacred spiritual places and public areas where the local people will take the responsibility and the initiative to make them bloom with beautiful flowers,' says Bishwajeet.

He draws another analogy, and says, 'I love my daughter. Therefore, I look after her, making sure she is well and fine. If we apply this caring and loving attitude to our streets, they can be transformed into places that look like they have been cared for and loved. This also applies to our language, our culture, our tradition, our family, our towns and villages and will help us thrive in the future.'

With thoughts of a hopeful future and an ownership of the leikai, I find myself in Ima Jamini's locality Khagenpalli Pankha, which is moving with the changing times. Ima Jamini's small house is neatly tucked into a corner, next to a palatial building. It looks warm and welcoming. The sprawling building in front of her house belongs to a police inspector. The aesthetically designed bungalow adjacent to hers is now dull and lifeless. The owner – a contractor and his family – fled to Bangalore after underground groups threatened him and hurled bombs at his house. Though the local Meira Paibis built a shed and stood vigil to protect them, they left the place. The residents seem to have succumbed to pessimism and a sort of silence has pervaded the area ever since.

She looks pensive when I ask her if she has ever faced similar problems. 'As elderly women, we don't think we have enemies. Everyone treats us with respect.' However, she recalls the days when there were no tall unfriendly walls. Today, every courtyard in the leikai is separated by bamboo fences, hedges and bamboo wickets.

There was a time when people living in the locality shared close ties. There were small openings in the hedges and neighbours could walk in anytime for an afternoon chat or to share a special curry or sweet dish cooked for lunch. On a lighter vein, a Meitei friend tells me, 'We are five sisters. Our father did not mind the low and hollow gate till we were in our teens. But the more years we added, the more sure he made that the walls became taller and the gates more opaque. The boys had to do all kinds of acrobatics to look at us!'

On a more serious note, tall walls and enclosures are created out of fear, anxiety and mistrust. 'The situation is getting worse every day and I don't blame the common people for fearing for their lives. Fear has been ingrained into our genes now,' Jamini points out.

As I push open the medium-sized iron gates to her house, I see an unused car rotting in a corner. Ima Jamini looks a little sleepy as she wakes up from her afternoon siesta. Her grandchild tugs on her phanek. Perhaps it's not the right time to visit her, but it's too late to change it, and so I go in.

As I glance around, I can see that she is an enterprising woman. There are two pigs near the pond at the back of the house. She has a small farm in her household where she runs a piggery and a poultry farm. A small patch of bright orange turns out to be a marigold flower sprawl in her front yard. It seems like it was planted rather hastily, almost as an afterthought. A neat garden with assorted flowers is not a very common sight in Manipur.

Ima Jamini points to a patch of green herbs. 'This is also my special medicinal corner which has a natural cure for many ailments. I try to treat the common ailments myself and rarely go to the doctor,' she smiles. Almost all the houses in Manipur, including hers, are devoid of embellishments and trimmings like fancy curtains, rugs or cushions. The houses more or less have a makeshift look about them, almost as if every household is ready to pack and run!

I can hear Ima Jamini yelling at the ducks and chicken as they chase each other. Her grandchild runs after the ducks and chases them towards the pond in the backyard. Jamini walks up to a patch of brinjal plants and clears the weeds with a spade. She continues talking to me.

The name of Manorama rings in bitter memories as Jamini is from the same locality. In fact, Manorama is a niece (a cousin's daughter); she was born after Jamini got married. Jamini, who studied upto Class VIII was married to an assistant teacher at Keishamthong Ahenthem Tomba Primary School in 1965. When she was young, there were no English-medium schools as there were no teachers to teach English. Her initial years saw a lot of struggle as her father was a poor farmer. She helped augment the family income by selling vegetables. She would also weave to help her family.

Today, she is busy with her small farm – growing vegetables, running a small piggery and poultry farm. She has six children, three daughters, three sons. One son is a teacher, one a computer mechanic and a third works with the army. 'I have fulfilled one of my major duties – got all my daughters married,' she heaves a sigh of relief. Talking of her sons, she adds, 'My elder son, too, wanted to join the army but my husband did not allow him. He wanted him to be a teacher instead.'

This petite woman has been juggling her household chores and her life as an activist. She is Vice-president of the All Manipur Women Social Reformation and Development Samaj. She has been working for almost 30 years at the local level as a Secretary of the local Meira Paibi group. 'I want to economically empower the women of Manipur. If the local women want to take part in any protest march, I bear their travel expenses.' Recently, she took 30 women to stage a protest in solidarity with Irom Sharmila.

In the 50 years of her life, she has seen how AFSPA

has changed the lives of ordinary people. Initially, when she was young, she only heard about fisticuffs among the local youth, not so much about guns. Now she's appalled at how innocent people are routinely killed, raped and arrested under the shadow of AFSPA. She gets to know all this from the newspapers which her sons read to her. She has been an active campaigner of Nishabandh. There were times when her husband got annoyed as the household work suffered, but her mother-in-law tacitly supported her.

As we talk of the day of the protest, Jamini's son beckons me inside their living room to watch the video footage of the iconic protest on a television set which is perched on a wooden table. The room has a wooden sofa set, a centre table and a bed that is usually meant for guests who come for a night-stay.

Though I have seen photographs of the protest, it is my first time viewing the video footage. Shivers run down my spine as I hear the mothers yelling, 'Indian Army, Rape Us.' A few neighbours come and sit on the floor and join in the viewing. Jamini refuses to join us and sits quietly outside in the verandah.

I come out and sit next to her. She clasps my hand and is quiet for a while. 'Till very late in the day, I did not realize that it was the same Manorama who I knew who had been brutally killed,' she says. She went to the place where her dead body was lying. She started shaking when she saw the bullet-ridden body and came back to the Macha Leima office. She took part in the discussion there. It was an uneasy meeting. The women felt that they had done so much to demand repeal of the Act. They said politicians keep promising many things. But nothing seems to happen. 'It was time we did something,' she says. Ima Jamini tells me that in an insurgency-ravaged state, mothers can emerge as a shield – a protective umbrella. Mothers belong to neither party – the security people doing their job and insurgents are busy with theirs. 'As mothers, we belong to both the parties. We can think of a plausible solution,' she says. She squats at the edge of the stairs leading to the verandah and rests her shoulder against the grill gate. The verandah is surrounded by iron grills. I see a wooden bench on the verandah which has an assortment of stuffed toys on it. As a local leader, it was not a very difficult decision for her to make, she says. 'Once we are out of the house and are with women, we don't care about our family and mundane affairs. Ours is a community in itself. We don't care what husbands, sons or our daughters-in-law will think. We feel empowered to take our own decisions,' she says. Even so, to join in the nude protest was the hardest decision of her life. The night before the protest seemed endless. Her heart was filled with fear: what if she were killed or shot? 'We had decided that we would lie down and open our clothes if we were stopped,' she tells me. She did not ask her husband as he might have objected. With a heavy heart, she went out without informing anyone.

After the protest was over, she called her son Ch. Dinesh Singh from a Public Call Office (PCO) and asked him to get his son from school immediately. She cautioned him that there could be trouble. Her nervous son rushed to the school to fetch his son. He also got to know that curfew has been imposed. Her family members were aghast when they saw the footage of their mother protesting on a local television channel. Immediately, they set out to trace her.

It was noon by the time the protest ended. The police offered to drop the Imas home. The mothers refused. 'We can't sit in your vehicle,' a defiant Ima told them. Curfew was imposed soon after. Jamini had to come home on foot. Her family was anxiously waiting. Her husband told her that they were trying to trace her after they saw her protesting on television. Once home, everyone was silent. Her husband and her sons kept quiet. Nobody said anything at all day.

Ima Jamini believes in making clear statements through her work. Life did not freeze for her. She stuck to her social activities. She sometimes spends nights in her office. Her family is used to this. Initially, her husband was irked. He even went to her office once, checked the rooms and met the other women who stay there. This pacified him. 'He realized that I did it for the greater good of Manipur. Now, he does not object,' she smiles.

In fact, when she saw the newspaper clippings and the footage the next day, she thought her life was over.

Even today, she fears that the episode may be aired again by local channels – even though she was part of it, she could never bring herself to watch the entire footage. 'I don't want to watch it,' she says. She feels a sense of shame before the children. She never thought she would be able to do something like this. 'We did the protest to ensure that such incidents are not recast in the future. Such a protest too should not be repeated.' she says.

Ima Jamini despairs when she thinks about the futility of their protest. But she has a sense of satisfaction that although they could not fully achieve their goals, they did succeed in evacuating the Assam Rifles from Kangla and removing AFSPA from seven assembly sections. 'I think it's an achievement of the mothers,' she says.

She often goes to meet Manorama's family. As a local leader, she participates in meetings. Police come after them. Once she was also arrested and jailed for three months under the National Securities Act (NSA). However, all cases against her were withdrawn. 'The jailor provided the best facilities. But we missed our familes. And like all NSA detunes, we got a stipend of Rs 1500,' she says. Even in the jail, she and her associates shouted slogans to repeal the AFSPA. The jailor had to come and ask them to stop.

Ima Jamini has little faith in politics and politicians but she has a strong conviction that AFSPA has to go and she is prepared to work hard towards this end. As a mother, for her, this is the only way to peace. She has a rational theory about this. If the Act is repealed, citizens can have a strong voice against the underground groups too. And if such groups continue to commit excesses then the Act can be reinforced. 'It's all right if the security forces engage with the UGs. But, killing and torturing innocents and hurling bombs at residential areas is not acceptable. My anger is against both the parties,' she says. But, she points out that the UGs usually don't commit atrocities against women. 'We are ready to speak up if they do.' She goes on to add, 'The government is here to protect people. Its job is not to commit atrocities on the people. If security forces engage with insurgents, we have nothing to say.'

She misses the carefree and happy days of her youth. Everything was different: 'The shops were open late, cinema halls screened shows till late, we would walk back home. Things began to change in the 1960s and people started to be killed. I'm not scared for myself actually, it's my daughters I'm scared for, my daughters and all the daughters of Manipur.'

Ima Jamini is busy all the time I'm with her. She moves around constantly, and I follow her everywhere, even when she walks to the pigsty and drags the black pig to the pond for a drink. He's a rather lazy pig and he comes back and lies down on a patch of grass. Ima Jamini chides him gently but to no effect. She continues to talk as she works and I find that she is really disturbed by the way things are. She's often unable to sleep at night for worrying about what is happening to her once peaceful hometown. Now the future seems so bleak. She remembers her early years, how free they were, how they swam and played and climbed trees. 'Now we're even afraid of going out of the home.'

Indeed, she is like a 'man' in the neighbourhood. Her husband and sons hide any news of quarrels or altercations in the locality from her. They fear that she might rush to intervene. It's not difficult to believe her when she says she was once known as a 'daredevil'.

'Your wife thinks she is like a man. Do you agree?' I ask Naba Kumar, her husband who has been sitting quietly. He grins, 'Of course, I agree.'

9

Keisham Ongbi Taruni Devi, aka Ima Taruni

Binalakshmi Nepram often jokes before delivering a public speech, 'Many in India think we are closer to China than India. My reply to them is, 'The beautiful clothes that I wear are woven by women of our land. They are not made in China!"

As she steps into international conferences and meetings in her traditional phanek and enaphi, she is flooded with compliments. People flock around her, feel her clothes and admire the unique weaves of the fabrics she wears. Apart from her crusade to empower women survivors of armed conflict, she has also been, in a way, the brand ambassador for the Meitei outfit in India and abroad.

'I feel happy wearing our traditional clothes as in doing so I am honouring the women weavers who slog it out each day. I feel proud in procuring the finished cloth from the remotest of villages and some of them are made by our members,' she says. She works with women in over 300 villages across Manipur, Tripura and many parts of Northeast India.

Her initiative, Manipur Women Gun Survivors Network (MWGSN), engages and empowers hundreds of women. A gender-sensitive approach to the gun crisis, it is an innovative first-of-its-kind initiative in India, its main agenda to give a healing touch to women and children caught in conflict situations. The network was formally launched on 26 April 2007 in Manipur's capital, Imphal.

She chose Leihao, a beautiful flower grown in Manipur, as a brand logo for the product line made by women gun survivors – traditional handlooms, handicrafts and paintings. 'This flower connotes purity. In Manipur, this flower is usually offered to gods and goddesses to usher in peace and prosperity in society. Moreover, women in Manipur wear Leihao in their hair to express happy moments.'

Elegantly dressed in her traditional attire, Binalakshmi has emerged as one of the most visible commentators on conflict in Northeast India on national television, social media and various women and disarmament meetings in the United Nations headquarters in New York. She has won several accolades for her work. However, the accolades have not altered her priorities. Her determination to usher in a change in her home state remains strong. Growing up in the 1980s in Manipur, she has seen what prolonged conflict can do to people's lives. The day she was born, there was curfew in Imphal. 'I now joke with friends that not even an army curfew could stop me from coming to this world,' she laughs.

Growing up was fun with four sisters and three brothers. She has fond memories of their home, Heirangoithong, where she grew up. But then, her young mind was scarred by a massacre in her locality, now famous as the Heirangoithing massacre of 1984 where 13 civilians were shot dead by the CRPF jawans.

Their home, however, was like a cocoon. Her father Nepram Bihari, was a government servant. But he was also a writer and an artist. He nurtured his children well and introduced them to the joy of reading encyclopedias, short stories and novels. The siblings used to spend hours in the children's section in the State Central Library reading and selecting books. He also ingrained a love for good films in the kids. 'He took us to watch the film *Killing Fields* based on the Cambodian genocide when I was only ten years old. I visited Cambodia in April 2006 and it brought back strong memories of the scenes that I saw in the film,' Binalakshmi recalls.

Unlike most other Meitei households, the kids missed their mother not being at home. Her mother Yensembam Ibemhal, a zoologist by training from Gauhati University, was a teacher. 'It was much later that I realized the values of what it is to be a working mother.' She was very good in Mathematics and Science and taught all her kids the basics of these two subjects. In fact, Ibemhal even published a geometry book in the early 1980s. This is one of Binalakshmi's prized possessions.

When young, Binalakshmi ventured out to Delhi for higher studies. She went first to Delhi University and then to Jawaharlal Nehru University (JNU), it was here that she realized that her life was different. 'As I grew up in this region, I thought all the violence and bloodshed I saw around me was natural. It was only after I came to New Delhi that I realized that it was not. Here, people kill each other for lack of parking space,' she laughs. As a young student, she kept track of the events back home and realized women were the worst sufferers in any conflict situation. Binalakshmi's work station is spacious – stretching from Delhi to remote parts of the northeast. Her pet project remains the Manipur Women Gun Survivors Network (MWGSN), which engages and empowers hundreds of women.

A disturbing incident triggered MWGSN. Binalakshmi had witnessed the aftermath of the killing of 27-year-old Buddhi Moirangthem in Wabgai Lamkhai village of Manipur's Thoubal district. There, a group of three gunmen had dragged Buddhi from his car-battery workshop. Within a matter of minutes they shot him dead. Till date, his young wife Rebika Akham does not know who the killers were and why they killed her husband. Binalakshmi was saddened by this senseless killing. She realized that only economic empowerment can provide succour to the distraught widow. She contributed Rs 4,500 (USD 110) to buy a sewing machine for Rebika Akham. This sewing machine changed Rebika's life. It enabled her to sew and tailor clothes for the villagers and earn a decent living after the death of her husband. This intervention was the game changer.

The Network has been working relentlessly to help women like Rebika, whose lives have been affected by gun killings of the bread earner of the house – usually a husband, father or son. They were victims of attacks either by the state or non-state actors. The one-point agenda of the Network is to support women in terms of the trauma faced in armed conflict and help them find ways to heal the scars. It helps women gun survivors to open bank accounts and provide small loans of Rs 3,000 to 9,000 (USD 75 to 225). 'With the help of this seed amount, these women can carry on work related to silk reeling, weaving and other occupations such as fishery or mushroom farming,' she tells me. They also form 'Solidarity Networks' of committed young people to help the survivors and control the use and spread of small arms.

The network is expanding. The Northeast India Women Initiative for Peace was formulated in 2010. It is a forum of women leaders from across the eight states of Northeast India, across ethnicities, who have vowed to work together for peace. Binalakshmi can be combative whenever there is a discussion on the AFSPA. I listen as the she tells me, 'We will need to reclaim our peace. These wars, killings, military operations have to stop in Manipur and the Northeast.'

The idea of reclaiming your own peace lingers with me as I make my way to Ima Taruni's home – her address Top-Khongnamakhong sounding like a tongue-twister – on the outskirts of Imphal city, an almost rural setting. The area is known for its enterprising people engaged in wood carving and cane work. Women are especially skilled in weaving handloom and the art of preparing *kabok* (ladoos made of powdered rice and jaggery). Evening was setting in as we threaded through winding roads to Taruni's home.

Taruni's life has always been a tussle. To begin with, there was an altercation between her grandparents over her name. Her grandfather wanted to name her Taruni (meaning neat) and her grandmother wanted to call her Mangolnganbi (which means 'queen of the house'). So serious were their differences on this, that they stopped talking to each other. And eventually, they died without having broken that deadlock. This left a deep impact on her. She tried to balance the disagreement in her own way. She was called Mangolnganbi in her parental home and later Taruni in her in-laws' house.

Her seven-year-old grandson listens as the 78-year-old woman starts sobbing as she describes how she had to toil through her childhood. She has a beautiful lined face and an air of tranquil confidence. Taruni tells me that her father was a wastrel, an irresponsible man. He had no time for his family, and was always engrossed in the game of betting on pigeon and dove fighting (a kind of traditional gambling).

Taruni, the eldest child, was burdened by familial responsibilities from early childhood. She is older by eight years than her two brothers. Her mother was so sick that she could not breastfeed her youngest brother. Taruni had to carry her brother to the neighbouring homes so he could suckle. The tradition of shared breastfeeding was prevalent that time, though it's not so frequent now. 'It ensures a better chance of survival for every child born in the community. Whenever necessary the women of the neighbourhood help in tending the child, giving relief to the mother. Nowadays, mothers prefer to bottle-feed their babies,' she tells me. In the bargain, Taruni had to help them in their household chores, cleaning utensils, and grinding paddy.

She had to run around doing all household chores and so she was forced to drop out of school quite early, at the primary level. She gets wistful as she recalls the few days she had spent in school. It was a primitive method of schooling. There were no desks or benches to sit on. She had to take a sack, sit on the floor and write with a chalk on a slate.

'Instead of going to school, my nimble little fingers were involved in intricate weaving,' sighs Ima Taruni. She used to weave to help the family. The paltry money she earned was used to send her brother to school. Her parent's home was at Khongman in Imphal East. She tells me, 'I wish I could have had some basic education. Maybe, my life would have been different. I could have read so many books. I would have known more about the world.'

Silhouetted in the light of the hurricane lamp, her face is remarkably composed. Evenings in Imphal see darkness before it comes naturally because of the regular load shedding. As she sits on the traditional *kauna* mat, Ima Taruni tells me that her house is more than 100 years old. She came here as a bride when she was barely 15. This is the house where she brought up eight children – five sons and three daughters.

She did not have a happy marriage, she tells me. Her husband, Keisham Lalabi, who used to work with the Manipur Rifles, was an alcoholic; he had seven wives, and used to beat Taruni regularly. I listen, as this feisty leader of the Nishabandh movement tells me about her abusive, alcoholic husband. And how she bore it all. I realize how deeply-embedded patriarchal notions are in the community when I hear this ancient Meitei saying, 'Nupigiluhongbadi Amuktani Nupadi Chamarak hongba yai' – 'A female can be married only once, but a male can marry hundred times.'

Taruni, with her wizened skin, is almost like a time capsule: she has seen Manipur change – from a tranquil 'land of gems' to a bloody land now. She has seen the tussle between cultures – one phase where the elderly and the children respected each other and now, when the situation has completely changed. At that time there were a few quarrels between local people and the elders were called in to negotiate. Today there are rampant killings by armed groups.

She feels there is a need to revamp the administrative system and blames the state as well as the central government for failing to give them jobs. It is this, she feels, which has pushed young people towards taking up arms – they're frustrated and have nothing to do. She has been camping in their usual place, the Planning and Development Agency (PDA) complex as part of the 'Save Sharmila' campaign. She explains why Irom Sharmila is fasting. 'She could not bear the killing of her brothers and the rape of her sisters. The AFSPA gives a blank cheque to the security forces. The Act has to be repealed in order to usher in normalcy in the state. The UGs too might calm down. Now everyone has lost their balance – the security forces as well as the UGs,' she says.

I smile as she talks about Delhi, and tells me that it is a much better place to live in. 'Give us land in Delhi where there is no AFSPA. We had once staged a protest in Delhi. But it was so peaceful. There were no security guards to keep an eye on us,' she says.

Manorama's death enraged her. She was shocked and she decided she had to do something about it. She saw Manorama's mutilated body in the RIMS morgue. She participated in the public outcry over the incident and also bore the brunt of teargas shells. She was part of the meeting that decided the extraordinary protest. She felt that she could do it. Rather, she had to do it. She joined in. 'When I rushed to the Kangla fort, a handsome officer said 'Maaji Namaste'. But, when we started stripping, the shocked officer left the scene,' she says.

The Manipur of her dreams is a peaceful society – where people live and eat together. If the violence continues, she feels that the Manipuri society will greatly suffer. She has the same kind of anger against both the UGs and the security forces – both kill innocents.

She had made a quiet resolve to safeguard the children of Manipur till her last breath. Her nagging knee pain does not deter her from sticking to this. She only has to hear of an incident of violence or shooting and she rushes to help. One time she landed up in jail for two months after she protested the illegal detention of a young boy by the Assam Rifles. She staged a hunger strike and the police picked up the strikers. In jail, she scoffed at the food, throwing the watery dal away to protest against the poor quality food served there.

Normally mild and courteous, Taruni can turn into a fury when the situation demands it. One time, during a relay hunger strike, a group of commandos came to threaten those sitting on strike. She confronted them and asked them to kill her. They pointed a gun at her. She then told them that she would count till three and then they could shoot her. They left, murmuring, 'This old woman is different.' Taruni then rushed out and stood in front of their vehicle. She challenged, 'You run me down and say it was an accident.' They were shocked. They quickly reversed their jeep and sped off.

She says she has no fear of speaking up and protesting if she is wronged, even if it means pelting stones at the security personnel. Indeed, she's been known for her fierce temper ever since she was a child. Whenever she was angry as a child or a young woman, she would starve herself. According to her, Sharmila's fast cannot be compared to Mahatma Gandhi's fasts, as he would at least drink water. Sharmila has not even done that. Her determination is much stronger than that of the man who is known as the father of the nation. She's also keen to know about everything that's going on in the world, but she can't read, so she asks her friends to read the newspaper to her. 'I have heard about the ethnic conflict in Sri Lanka,' she tells me. I am amazed at her knowledge of global affairs.

Domesticity sits easily with her activism somehow. Taruni manages her many roles with seeming ease. She is many characters rolled into one – a doting grandmother, a gentle woman, and a fiery activist. Not surprisingly, her son is unhappy at this. 'For her,' he says, 'the problems of the society are more important. She's hardly ever at home. And whenever I think of the nude protest by my mother and her friends, I feel sad.'

People are surprised by the way she responds to issues. Once there was a fire in a house in the locality and in the scramble, a small boy was stranded in the burning house. She tried to rush in, but some men stopped her. She then persuaded one of the men to go in and rescue the child while the others stood in a queue with buckets of water to douse the fire.

Ima Taruni believes she has a task to perform and as long as she is alive, she will continue to do so. As she sits with her grandchildren, she spanks one of them and laughs, 'I don't expect much from the younger generation. They are all afraid to die.'

10

Angom Jibanmala, aka Ima Jibanmala

It is a moment of silent pride as Lin Laishram looks at her own image at the huge billboard in New York's John F. Kennedy International Airport. For a moment, she finds herself transported to the pocket-sized yet heavily guarded airport in her hometown Imphal. Lin, a young girl of nine, peers at the shifty eyes of the security personnel. As she shuffles her shoes, she can see the paws of the huge sniffer dog. For a moment, the little girl is startled. She sits down in one of the chairs meant for passengers and starts reading the signboards. A big one reads 'security check'. She feels reassured only after her father Laishram Chandrasen, an avid sports buff, comes and sits next to her.

Lin, training to be an archer, encouraged by her father, had been packed off to Jamshedpur for advanced training at the Tata Archery Academy. Playing at the national level, she bagged the Junior Championship

Title in Chandigarh, but then an accident cut short her brief career in archery. Little did the budding archer from Imphal imagine then that she would one day be a model and actor and see herself on American billboards.

It's been a long journey, both geographically and psychologically. For her, 'Growing up was not easy with fear and violence all around. All parents wanted to send their kids out,' she tells me. While she was studying Sociology at Sophia College, Mumbai, she was exposed to ideas that were perhaps not traditional fare in her hometown. She admits that modelling was never a preferred choice in her family. It is not considered a good career for a girl from a middle-class family. Her mother wanted her to be an academic. She smiles, 'But, I was different. I always had a bit of an actor and an entertainer in me. I was the entertaining child in the house.'

It is a lovely Saturday afternoon when I meet with Lin. The brightness of her voice strikes me as special. When I ask about her name, her soft eyes light up as she laughs, 'My friends could not pronounce my name. Gradually, from Linthoingambi Laishram, I metamorphosed into Lin Laishram.'

Lin has been a wanderer all her life. After Mumbai, she had a four-year stint in New York. As she talks about her life behind the lights and camera in an alien land, she tries to weave in memories of her past – her early life in Imphal, then Mumbai and then New York and back to Mumbai. A personal visit to New York was a tipping point in more ways than one. The 5'9" attractive model with 'exotic looks' was an instant hit in the fashion world. She was cast by a jewellery company and things started rolling. She made the most of her stay in New York, participating in various shows.

But she'd always wanted to be an actor, and so she enrolled herself for acting classes at the Stella Adler Studio of Acting in New York and participated in various workshops on acting. As she began to move more seriously into the world of acting, she shuttled between New York and Mumbai and did workshops with a company called Prabha Theatre Laboratory, and even worked in actor Naseeruddin Shah's theatre group Rangbaaz.

Lin was attracted by the magic of Bollywood but with her 'oriental' looks she found she could work both in India and abroad. She explains that the market is narrow for a person with mongoloid features, especially in a context where conventional good looks mean having big eyes. It was thus easier for her to enter the world of television commercials and the fashion ramp, both of which loved her looks.

She dabbled in Hindi cinema by playing a small role in the film *Om Shanti Om*. She had also auditioned for the lead role in the Bollywood film *Mary Kom*, a biopic based on the world boxing champion M C Mary Kom, which went on to garner both critical and commercial acclaim, but she did not get the lead role, although she did manage the role of the boxer's friend and sparring partner. 'I don't have any complaints,' she says. 'Questions were raised about why they cast an actor who was racially so different. It is about reaching out to the majority of Indians. Bollywood wants Priyanka Chopra.' But then, Lin was inspired by Chopra's energy and grit. 'She is so hard working. I have not seen actors like her in the northeast,' she tells me.

Lin is also happy that someone like the director Sanjay Leela Bhansali had the far-sightedness to go to Manipur and plan to make a big-budget movie. 'We have been outcast for so long. Nobody knows where Manipur is. We should think positive,' she smiles.

As we conversed, Lin shared many anecdotes about her modelling stints with big names like Tarun Tahiliani and Shantanu-Nikhil and the Kingfisher calendar. While in New York, nobody believed that she was Indian, almost everyone mistook her for a fairer version of an African American. She did many international shows. 'That was fun, darken the skin and wear a wig. Sometimes I was mistaken for a Russian (Siberian). Some thought I was Turkish. I loved playing chameleon all the while,' laughs Lin.

Lin has a deep affection for her home state, Manipur. She keeps the narrative moving. 'When I talk to people, I tell them about Manipur, its rich culture and tradition. I would google and show them my state. I have a deep connection with Manipur. I feel my Manipuriness comes out in everything I do. My cultural values are very Manipuri,' she says. While traditions are important, Lin has also walked the ramp in Manipuri fashion shows. She developed an interest in the traditional textiles of her state and has made a documentary on textile traditions too. In order to do this, she did a great deal of research and now intends to do a PhD on the subject. 'It is still on the backburner,' she smiles.

New York and Mumbai gave her what Manipur could not – a home where she could be herself. Having lived independently in big metros and cities for a long time, it has become difficult to come back to a small town. She would like to work on Manipur but thinks that she would find it difficult to settle down here. 'When it comes to work I need to be independent. When everybody is worried about your whereabouts and safety, it kills the joy,' she says.

Lin longs for peace in her home state and she has a personal solution for this peace. It's love. She feels that if people begin loving their state, their culture, things will sort themselves out. She cites the example of Mahatma Gandhi who translated this anger into a positive energy through love. Irom Sharmila would not have put her life on the line if she did not love her state and her people.

'We need to communicate and know what we want. Violence brings only sorrow. Hopefully, our children and grandchildren will start thinking about peace. Each of us will have to contribute. If we do something bad, it creates a ripple effect. We have the power to change the world. We will have to direct our energies towards peace. Each of us is responsible for a sustainable future for our next generation. Our action begins with taking care of our thoughts for a healthy society,' she says.

Hidden somewhere between the gory and bloody stories and headlines of Manipur are stories like that of Lin Laishram. Lin admits that she owes her exhilarating journey to her supportive Ima, who gave her the freedom to try new things in life.

Her affirmative story transports me to the life of another happy woman, Ima Angom Jibanmala in Imphal. At 55, Jibanmala is a cheerful woman. Married to a hard-working man who owns a stationery shop, a fairly successful business, they live in a two-storeyed house at a locality called Uripok Sinam Leikai in Imphal. 'We saved every paisa to build this house,' she says with a sense of pride.

I perch myself on a plastic chair in the long winding verandah on the ground floor of their house. My somewhat sudden visit has upset her plans – she is impatient, as she is dressed and ready to go out. But she entertains me – to start with, she calls up someone on her mobile phone asking for glasses of juice for us. I am amused at the ways people use technology – she used her phone to speak to someone in the same house, I find out as I see her daughter, Juliet, walk down the stairs with a tray with glasses of pineapple juice. Jibonmala smiles, 'She works as a nurse in a private hospital. She doesn't talk much. I have to get her married now.'

Jibonmala loves talking about her family. She feels that of her children her younger son is the more responsible one. He runs a grocery shop, is married and with two children. But her eldest, who is an actor, is a bit of a worry. He plays the role of a villain in Manipuri films. He is still struggling and is yet to get married. 'He was in a rock band earlier. Some film producers noticed him. He enjoys acting. But I wish he would settle down. And I don't like him being a villain. One day, I want him to play the hero's role as the sympathy always lies with the hero,' she laughs.

So how does she see the armed forces – as heroes or villains? 'Oh, they are worse than villains,' she says. For the past six months now, she has been staying at the Planning and Development Agency (PDA) complex and participating in the relay hunger strike titled 'Save Sharmila'. 'I envy the indomitable spirit of Sharmila and her strong will. She is like an incarnation of God and not another human being like us,' she says.

She recalls a hilarious incident when a group of commandos and one plain-clothes man came near the tent where they were sitting on hunger strike. One of these women saw them at a distance. They were whispering, almost conspiring among themselves. The man in plain-clothes started running and the commandos ran after him pretending that they were chasing a militant and would shoot him. The women kept looking and laughing at them, knowing very well that it was just a ploy to make them come out of the tent so that the security forces could dismantle it. 'We are smarter than them. We fooled them by sitting inside the tent and laughing at them,' she says, laughing at the memory.

The solidarity of these women is admirable. Once during a storm at night the asbestos sheet blew off but they sat huddled together, even though it rained all night. She points out how some security men are scared of them. 'One day we had a candlelight vigil in front of Sharmila's photo. A convoy of three vehicles stopped there and the men got out and bowed their heads. Maybe they thought it was a temple,' she laughs again. But she agrees that all the commandos are young kids with no respect for anyone. They have to pay a hefty bribe when they are inducted into the forces. She is happy that none of her sons wants to join the security forces or the underground groups.

With the mobile phone hung around her neck, a bag on her shoulder, she is all set to go to the spot where the other women are waiting for her. In a shopping bag, she has a change of clothes. She is wearing rubber shoes to beat the rain. She need not worry about her house as her daughter-in-law and daughter are there to take care of it. 'My husband is very co-operative and understands that I have to keep myself busy. We do have fights occasionally like any normal married couple,' she smiles.

Earlier, Jibonmala used to do embroidery to help her husband. 'Now I find it difficult due to old age. I have no time to help him in his shop either,' she says. Activism is almost like a post-retirement vocation for her – retirement from her household chores and day-to-day responsibilities. For her, the trigger point was the way Manorama was killed, which she feels is an affront to the dignity of women. 'I saw the dead body of Manorama. I was very disturbed. It was terrible. We are all Manorama's mothers,' she says. Her friends, who were with her at the time, were hysterical. 'We wanted to do something that would shake the establishment. We signed a pact to disrobe ourselves. After I saw the body, it was not all that difficult for me to strip. I was agonized: how could someone be brutalized so much,' she says.

After the iconic protest, she did not faint. A journalist dropped her home in a car with another protestor, Momon, who stays in the same locality. 'All of us were crying. I felt embarrassed about coming back.' But nobody in her family talked about it. Sometimes she hears people sniggering behind her back. 'When newspapers flashed our photo, I felt violated. But I felt it was also important to highlight our cause in the media,' she says.

Fortunately, nobody in her family has been tortured or killed. But she has always been active in social causes – especially the drive against alcoholism. 'So many things keep happening in Manipur that I could not stay silent or away from it,' she says.

She recalls other similar incidents. Sanamacha, a school student was taken by the army for questioning but never came back. 'As a mother, at times I feel life is not worth it. I feel that there is a need to respond to the current situation,' she says. She studied up to class X but she makes it a point to read the local language newspaper every day. She also watches television news, both local and national, to keep herself abreast of what's happening.

But does she have the same anger against the UGs? She responds wisely, 'Now it's come to a point that we are sandwiched. Once, the UGs killed a woman called Menaka. The outfit declared that she was an army informer. That is why she was killed. But if we protest against them, we get warnings. We, the Meira Paibis, are here to protect the people. We are stuck in between. We are not here to take sides,' she says. She was disturbed by reports of recruitment of child soldiers by the UGs. 'I believe it's wrong to train children. If somebody has attained maturity, it's not possible to stop them. We issued press releases on this,' she says.

But like any mother, she is concerned about her family, especially her sons. She wishes her sons would get into government service but she feels that she won't be able to afford to buy the jobs by paying bribes. For now she enjoys watching her son's films. He is quite popular and his name is James Angom. 'He looks so real as a villain that I want to bash him. Come to think of it, he is such a gentle soul otherwise. He does not raise his voice nor does he smoke or drink,' she says.

She adds that he looks perfectly normal without the garish make-up and eyebrows. Her only hope is that he brings a bride on his own. 'I don't have time to look for one. If the bride's father asks, I will have to tell them that he is a villain,' she laughs. But she will make it a point to tell the bride's family that this villain's mother is also a bold Meira Paibi.

She looks up as the pigeons start their soft throaty cooing. The pigeons have made their nest on the tree in her courtyard. I smile as she tells me, 'The story of Manipur is too long to end in one conversation. We are notorious women. We have a lot of stories to tell.'

11

Laishram Gyaneswari, aka Ima Gyaneswari

The fading yellow walls in the room tell many stories. They tell me the tale of a child who wanted to grow up and see the world. A 13-year-old's wall scribblings with his gel pen. There are black and white pencil sketches too. A sketch of a motorcycle minus a rider. Next to it is a sketch of a convertible racing car, picked up from television or some glossy sports magazine. The third picture is of a boy going to school with a bag on his shoulders which says 'Go to school'.

My eyes drift towards the moist eyes of the wrecked mother who has been wailing inconsolably. Khoijam Medha's son went out to play after school and never came back. He has apparently been recruited as a child soldier by a militant outfit. Her son is not alone. Many other children have been enticed or coerced on some pretext or the other and recruited by militant outfits.

The outfits later declare that the children joined them of their own free will.

Towards the end of July 2008, I had set out to report on incidents of child soldiers being recruited by militant outfits in Manipur. Clad in salwar kameez, I stand out as an outsider amidst women in their traditional phanek and enaphi. I am ill-at-ease as curious onlookers watch me suspiciously. I see a house with smashed windowpanes. An eerie silence follows me as I walk through the narrow lane leading to a sparse courtyard surrounded by houses on four sides. I am near National Highway 39 in Manipur's Thoubal district. As I come closer, I hear a sobbing sound from within. I see a few women standing near the collapsible gate leading to the house.

Medha looks haggard. A purple phanek is tied carelessly around her waist. She wears a handwoven shawl over a white top. A few other women join her. She takes me into her living room which has a wooden sofa set and a centre table. There is one iron framed window with opaque panes. It's shut. The other one is open. There is no curtain, and a used, white Eveready battery is placed precariously on the windowsill. There is also a wooden study table with a few wooden chairs in the room. A white school uniform is slung on a chair, while a white tie with green stripes is carelessly tossed on top of the missing boy's textbooks that lie scattered on the table.

The mother fondly takes out his school bag and shows his books, his sketches and his colour pencils. I try to curb my emotions and ask the distressed mother the usual journalistic questions. It takes her some time to open up. The tears begin to tall again. Her voice trembles as she says, 'I urge the militants to release our children. My son is a bright student, he wants to join the Navy.' But she already knows she is waging a lost battle.

Recruiting child soldiers by militant outfits is not a new phenomenon. I read a report of the international NGO, Human Rights Watch, which mentions that an average child soldier is of the age group 13-17, while some are as young as eight or nine. Most are unwilling militants, abducted from their villages to serve as guerrilla fighters, or in supporting roles in armed conflicts in more than 50 countries. They bear arms in battle, serve as human mine detectors, participate in suicide missions and act as spies, messengers or lookouts. Common Article 3 of the Geneva Convention, 1949, places an obligation on both State and non-State actors in an internal armed conflict situation not to target women, children and non-combatants.

I am a bit torn, I'm here as a journalist in search of a story. I have a grieving mother sitting beside me, and I am meant to interview her. As I try to console her, I hear murmurs around me. Suddenly, I have an uncanny feeling – it's as if we're being watched, and indeed we are. As I look up I see eyes peering in from the windows. Reporting from a conflict zone can spring surprises at every step; it's one of those moments when I have a brush with fear. Security forces surround the house, one of the commanders comes in and starts hurling questions at Medha. He speaks to her in Meitei, so I can't decipher anything. He gives me a wary look and asks me for my identity card. I insist that I am a journalist, and he has a few discussions on the phone, presumably checking my credentials. He tells Medha in his native language that they thought that I was a 'mediator' trying to negotiate her boy's release. Handing over my identity card, he apologizes and leaves. I feel I have been holding my breath all the while and I heave a sigh of relief when he is gone. I am told that I am fortunate that at least they stopped to ask. Since the state is under AFSPA, the security forces have unrestricted and unaccounted power to carry out their operations once an area is declared disturbed. Even a non-commissioned officer is granted the right to shoot to kill based on mere suspicion that it is necessary to do so in order to 'maintain the public order.'

After I finish my interview and head back, I find myself still unnerved by the experience. One question continues to bother me – how did they get to know of my arrival when I had not discussed my travel plans with anyone?

My trips to Manipur are often brief, restricted to two to three days. I rush around and try to meet as many people as possible. I have always admired the resilience of the people there, especially the women. Back in my hotel room, I try to sleep, but Medha's pleading eyes haunt me. Even as I find myself helpless, I look forward to meeting another woman in the morning – one who embodies the resilient spirit of women in this state, Ima Gyaneswari, one of the nude protestors.

I draw the curtains, bleary-eyed, to see that the sun is out. After a quick breakfast of bread, butter, and a glass of juice in my hotel room, I start off early in the morning to meet Ima Laishram Gyaneswari. Imphal's Nagamapal Road is just waking up. It is a commercial area, most of the shutters are down. Some are half-open and a few men are sitting on the footpath brushing their teeth. I see some signboards on the way, including a Western Union money transfer one. A shop's signboard announces Information Technology Services, Web Hosting and Design, Human Resource Services and Business Consulting.

I approach a closed shop with the signboard Indo-Myanmar Furniture Shop – the address I was given. Just then, a man starts unlocking its wooden shutters. He smiles at me and surprises me by speaking in impeccable Hindi. Clad in a purple shirt and white pyjamas, he has a moustache and neatly-combed hair, and introduces himself as Fateh Chand Jain, proprietor of the shop and Ima Gyaneswari's husband. 'So, it's an inter-community marriage,' I say to myself. I am intrigued. I try to prod him further. He is calm. He starts looking at his account books and speaks to his assistant. He ushers me in. He is pleasant but cautious. He smiles, 'Why don't you ask her? I don't interfere in her matters.' He gestures to me to go through the door at the back of the shop which connects to his house. As I step through, I see a small courtyard with houses on all four sides. On one side of the courtyard is a two-storeyed house with a wooden ladder. The outer walls are not plastered, but there is a flurry of activity in the courtyard. Two scooters and a kinetic Honda are parked there and a few clothes are drying on the clothesline. I can see smoke coming out of the kitchen.

Fateh Chand makes me sit in their small living room adjacent to the shop, which opens onto a narrow verandah. It is sparsely decorated though it has sturdy and well-polished wooden furniture and a vase with red plastic flowers. I start chatting with him. He has no qualms in speaking about his Meitei wife who joined a dozen Manipuri Imas, mothers, on 15 July 2004, to stage the naked protest outside the Assam Rifles headquarters at Kangla Fort. He sits with me and recalls the day. He did not have any inkling of his wife's intentions. She left the house early. 'I heard about the unique protest in the afternoon from one of my fellow business associates. I had an inkling my wife might be involved. She had touched my feet before she left the house, something she usually does when she leaves for something important. But this time she didn't tell me where she was going. I'm very proud of her. Not everyone can be so brave, right?' he adds.

Ima Gyaneswari emerges with a *thali* for her *puja*. She looks fresh after an early morning bath. She is dressed in a yellow phanek, her head covered with a cream-coloured enaphi. She wears a white sandalwood bindi. She prostrates herself before the small temple, with tin doors and a tin roof, in the courtyard. She lights some incense and folds her hands and prays with her eyes closed.

Poised and graceful, she walks towards us. Her broad smile puts me at ease. She must have been very attractive in her youth, I can tell. A science graduate from Ghana Priya Women's College, Imphal, she was a spirited political activist as a student. After she married, she devoted her time to domesticity and taking care of her family. But she remained an active member of the local chapter of the Meira Paibi women's movement.

For a person like Ima Gyaneswari whose world revolved around her home, her Meira Paibi friends were her window to the world outside. She kept herself abreast of the happenings around her. She was emotionally stirred by the story of Chanu Rose, who was raped by security men back in the 1960s. 'The young girl could not take it and later committed suicide,' she recounts.

She is agonized by the horror stories of atrocities on women – several incidents of molestation, rape and torture by army men; even pregnant women are not spared, she says. 'All these stories pained me deeply.' Then there were the many young people taken away by army personnel, never to be seen again. 'I know of many mothers who have gone insane after their sons and daughters disappeared,' she tells me.

However, mothers like her lost their patience after Thangjam Manorama was taken into custody, never to return. 'Our Meira Paibi members saw her body being brought to the Regional Institute of Medical Sciences (RIMS), Imphal for the post-mortem, and they spread word about the incident. I was agonised when I heard. If this is what lies ahead for the young girls of Manipur, what will become of our community? We had to rise up to protect our girls,' says Gyaneswari.

Manorama's death led to a civil uprising. On 12 July 2004, 32 local organizations formed an umbrella organization called Apunba Lup, to launch a movement to demand repeal of the AFSPA. However, several mothers including Gyaneswari felt this was not enough. The dejected women gathered for a closed-door meeting on 13 July and deliberated on alternative ways of confronting the situation. She speaks slowly, 'It was a general feeling that we, the women of Manipur, were virtually naked. We could easily be molested or raped. Why then should we not walk in the streets naked? Why not tell the whole world about our helpless situation?'

The night seemed endless. Gyaneswari spent the entire night staring at the ceiling. She woke up early in the morning, took her bath, offered her prayers. 'I touched my husband's feet before I left,' she says. 'In my mind, I asked him to forgive me because I was going to do something very controversial. And I couldn't possibly tell him about it.' She left home at six in the morning.

She had often passed the gates of the Kangla fort. But on that day, the fort seemed distant and forbidding. By the time she reached its gates, 30 women had assembled there; 10 more trickled a little later. They were expecting some more women to gather, but time was running out. 'It was a vital moment. We could not afford to waste time. The security forces might get suspicious and impose a curfew,' narrates Gyaneswari. Steeling themselves to make a rush on the gate, the protestors did not realize that there were finally only 12 of them. 'I did not count the number of women then. I had no awareness of anything. I was in my own world, shouting slogans, screaming at the Indian army to rape us, take our flesh. All that filled my mind was the image of Manorama's corpse,' she recalls.

It was an angry moment. The mothers were incensed. Ima Gyaneswari grits her teeth as she speaks, 'We confronted the men in uniform with fire in our hearts. It was like the climax of the rage and agony we had harboured for years. We challenged them to come out and rape us before everyone. We urged that they tell us what they were stationed here for: to protect our people or to rape our women.'

I walk up the wooden ladder steps with Ima to the first floor of her house, where I meet her beautiful elder daughter Girija, sitting on the bed with her new-born baby. A white mosquito net with purple flowers woven with purple satin stripes hangs at one end of the bed. I am spellbound by the intricate mosquito nets in Manipur. Elaborately designed with satin, mosquito nets with a royal look are also a part of the wedding trousseau of a Meitei bride. They are locally stitched by tailors. Two mosquito nets go with the bride – one for the master bed and one for a single bed. The net is designed rather like the royal nets with four corners opened and hung on the four posts of a bed. And it is not pulled down and folded and kept away every day. It's a legacy of the royal family and noblemen of Manipur which some women's self-help groups decided to innovate and improvise on for the local market.

Ima Gyaneswari goes back to the day when she created history. She tells me how it was a difficult task to return home that day. She was edgy and restless. She was worried about how her family would react. 'I was shaking like a leaf,' she gives a nervous smile as she cuddles her grandchild, 'I had not sought my husband's permission.'

However, she was relieved when her husband reassured her that she had done something courageous. 'Whatever you have done is for the women of Manipur,' he told her. Gyaneswari's elderly mother, Laishram Gambhini, and her four children, also hugged her and told her how they were all stirred by her courage.

Girija has come to her mother's house with her newborn. 'My mother has inspired us to do something for our women. My mother's will power is very strong. I have never seen her weak or breaking down. She can face anything alone,' she says.

The dressing table in the room is cluttered with a lot of things, a bottle of Glucon D, moisturizing cream, a steel bowl, a bottle of water, a baby's teething ring, a pouch of yellow shampoo, a mobile charger, a plastic box full of lipsticks and nail polish, and a baby's diaper. Ima Gyaneswari kisses her grandchild. She knows that that their protest managed to hit international media headlines. The whole world was talking about it. But back home, things don't seem to change. The indifference of the state pains her. She closes her eyes. 'It is distressing. I do feel the armed forces are more cautious while dealing with women now. The acts of molestation, rape and torture have come down. But the inhuman crimes committed under the AFSPA's cover persist.'

We walk down the stairs. I hold on to the wooden handrails as Gyaneswari turns back and tells me, 'I am surprised that you have come here. Nobody bothered to come and meet us. Nobody cared to ask why the 12 mothers of Manipur had to stage such a protest.' She then sits near her elderly mother. Her mother is quiet, maybe because she can't speak in Hindi like her daughter. Ima smiles, and is the perfect host when she tells me, 'This is your home. Whenever you are in Imphal, do come and visit me.'

12

Ima Ningthoujam Sarojini, aka Ima Sarojini: Mother on the Go

I still remember the date. It was 10 May 2008, a warm afternoon. I look at my mobile phone to check the time. It is 4.45 pm. I put my phone on silent mode, and walk in as the tightly guarded collapsible gate slides opens for just a brief while.

I stand in the white-tiled room at the Special Isolation ward of Imphal's Jawaharlal Nehru Hospital. I stare, mesmerized, at the woman sitting on the adjustable hospital bed in front of me. So far, I have only read about her, seen her photographs. But today, here I am, face to face with Irom Chanu Sharmila, the woman who has been on an indefinite hunger strike since 2 November 2000, demanding repeal of the Armed Forces (Special Powers) Act from Manipur. I stand still as I look at the activist who has been on the world's longest hunger strike.

Irom Sharmila's story of defiance haunts everyone

who visits Manipur. A killing of ten civilians allegedly by security forces at a bus stop in Malom, a town in Manipur, stirred this young girl's mind. Among those killed was Sinam Chandramani, a 1988 National Bravery Award winner. Sharmila was 28 when she took a vow that she would go on a fast, and would not eat until the AFSPA was repealed. Three days after she started her fast, she was arrested by the police and charged with 'attempt to commit suicide', an unlawful act under the Indian Penal Code section 309.

Later, she was sent to judicial custody. After a few days, on 21 November 2002, the authorities decided to keep Sharmila alive through force-feeding by implanting a nasogastric intubation, a tube through which she was fed liquids. Every year, they release her and then re-arrest her, so that they stay within the provisions of the law which states that a person who 'attempts suicide shall be punished with simple imprisonment for a term which may extend to one year (or with fine, or with both)'.

There is a raw energy about Sharmila. As I stand, still wonderstruck to be in her presence, she smiles and says, 'I am happy to see you.' She seems genuinely happy to see me, and this breaks the ice. I pull up a plastic chair, sit near her bed and smile back at her. She has a neatly decorated corner by her bedside where she has stuck on the wall, greeting cards and paintings sent to her by her well-wishers. There is a stack of books and some potted plants on the windowsill.

As far as I can remember, I have always seen Irom Sharmila in various arresting images. And invariably, her uncombed curly hair was open as if it had a mind of its own. In fact, I realize, I have never seen her with her hair tied up. I ask her, 'Why do you always leave your hair open?' I listen as she tells me in an unhurried tone, 'Until my demand is fulfilled, I will not comb my hair. I don't even use a mirror. It's part of my determination. It's more important as it reflects my mind as well. I don't want to compare myself with the past. There are some changes in my physical appearance. I think it will help me to keep my ego in check.'

It's rather odd to conjure up an image of the legendary character Draupadi in the midst of the pungent odour of disinfectant and antiseptic, but my mind goes back to the *Mahabharata*, and the angry Draupadi who took a vow that she would not oil or tie her hair until she could wash it with the blood of Dushasana, after he was killed.

I listen to Sharmila's vow. I have travelled far and wide, from glitzy cities to quiet countrysides, but this frontier state and its people have always left me mesmerized. I have often tried to locate Manipur in terms of essential experiences and looked for ways to get under its skin. I spent a fruitful two hours with the Iron Lady of Manipur at the special isolation ward. Inside the secluded high security ward, Irom Sharmila patiently waits to achieve the goal she has set herself. And the wait has been ceaseless. She does get bored, but she is always calm. She smiles again, 'Every 15 days I go to the court. It has become normal routine for me. Sometimes, I do find it dull.'

Without warning, she stands up. Probably, she is tired of sitting on the bed. She begins to pace up and down the room and in the corridor outside. I keep looking at her. Pointing to the pipe fitted to her nostrils, she smiles again, 'This pipe has become a part of my body now. Even my nostrils have enlarged over the years.'

Behind the kind and gentle demeanour lies a feisty spirit, and an artistic soul. I did not know that Sharmila is also a poet. When I visit her, she tells me she has been writing a poem and that she has also thought of a title for it – 'Administration'. 'It's going to be long poem based on certain principles I believe in. I have already written 13 pages,' she says. She reads out one stanza. 'It's written in my mother-tongue and so it's somewhat difficult for me to translate and explain it in English. It's very tough. My English is very poor.' I smile and gently prod her to read me one or two of her poems.

Sharmila has been writing poems since 1999. She has written about little events that struck a chord with her or made her cry. 'Writing poems was my means of doing something worthwhile as a living being. I try to express myself in words to the best of my ability,' she says. Her first poem was titled 'Take away the chain from my ankle'. 'I wrote this poem from the perspective of a lame bird, as I felt like one myself. I was around 26 years old then.' But she does not recall where she had kept her first poem. 'The poem, maybe it's at home. Maybe it's lost. I don't know.'

We keep going back and forth between the past and the present. She talks about her childhood. I ask her, 'Were you different or extraordinary as a child?' She laughs, 'I was as simple and ordinary as other children. I am the youngest in my family. In all, we are nine. I was somewhat pampered. I was very close to my eldest brother who passed away on 7 June 1997. I was close to my sisters also. But my ideology blended more with my eldest brother. In fact, he was a source of inspiration for me.' However, she was not very close to her mother. 'My mother was too busy running a grocery shop,' she tells me.

Spending long days and nights in an isolation ward in a hospital could not have been easy. I ask her, 'Which part of the day do you like the best?' She responds, 'I like midnight the best. At night time, I am at peace with myself. Right now I am in the battlefield. During the day, I am very anxious. Moreover I feel disturbed by the passers by who stare at me, as if I am some kind of an alien species in the zoo. But it's fine here. I don't want to go outside the gate.'

She walks down memory lane with me and tells me that her childhood was quite normal. She enjoyed doing all the normal household chores that every young girl was supposed to do. She smiles again. 'I liked doing everything. Cooking was my favourite pastime.'

She grew up to be a strong woman, like most women in Manipur. 'Yes, our women are quite powerful. They can dedicate their lives for the good of society very easily. There are so many examples.' I tell her how much she is admired all over the world. 'Are you an example of the strength of a Manipuri woman?' I ask her. She smiles again. She hopes the younger generation can learn something about endurance and willpower from her. She's also optimistic, hopeful. She reassures me, 'The future is in the hands of God. I am not religious but have full faith in God.' But there is no particular God that she believes in. 'It's the almighty. I can't see his form nor can I hear his voice. But he is there. He is guiding me and is my source of inspiration.'

We meander and talk about a host of things. Sharmila is worried about the future of Manipur. 'It will be brighter after the realization of my demand. I feel I have somewhat been able to inspire the youth.' She is however, oblivious of the global attention she's getting. It doesn't mean much to her.

She preaches the message of peace, even to the underground groups (UGs). 'Demands can never be fulfilled through weapons. All demands should emerge from sincerity, perseverance, dedication and love.' She also opposes the government's move to arm villagers to protect themselves. She urges both the state and the non-state actors not to be 'war-mongers'.

We come back to our lives. She tries to wave off a

mosquito. 'There are a lot of mosquitoes. Every day, I use a mosquito repellent and a mosquito net at night,' she tells me. And what does all the graffiti and the photographs on the walls of the hospital room mean? She smiles, 'I don't know how to express myself. These things inspire my day-to-day life.'

She then looks at the time. She smiles, 'My watch is very important. Time keeps me going and keeps my mind clear. I keep looking at the watch all the time.'

The timekeeper reminds me of my own schedule. I have a meeting with Ima Sarojini, who I have missed meeting on two earlier occasions. She is the mother-on-the-go, almost never at home. On the way to her home I cross several big buildings. I stop near the house. Plastered with mud, it is a house made with reed, and I can see a hand pump and a few women collecting water there.

Ima Sarojini is nowhere to be seen. A young girl comes out and introduces herself as Sarojini's daughter. Her name is N Bala. She lives next door with her family. She has come to see her father who is not well. She tells me, 'Mother's just left. Anyway, she is never home.' She then speaks about their 'troubled' family, she tells me her mother is involved with the Universal Mother's Organisation (UMO), an NGO and that she spends most of her time in the office. It's on rare occasions that she comes home.

Bala tells me, 'My father used to work as a constable with the Manipur Rifles, in the police department. Two of my siblings died from illness and one drowned. After that, my father went into depression and stopped going to office. Later he was suspended from his job.' She then adds, 'We had a lot of ancestral property but everything has been sold off now.'

I almost feel like an intruder as Ima Sarojini's husband, 62-year-old Ningthoujam Tamar Singh, comes out to look at me. He asks his daughter about me. When he comes to know that I am a journalist, he starts pouring his heart out. He asks me, 'Can you write about my miserable life? I managed to build this makeshift house by the side of a hill. I know we will be evicted soon as this is *khas* (state-owned) land.' He starts grumbling. 'Can you imagine, in this big state of Manipur, I have no land that I can call my own? If evicted maybe we will have to live on the streets. I have worked as a rickshaw puller and even as a chowkidar,' he sighs.

I ask him about his wife. And he sounds angry. 'Oh, she is a VIP. She is a busy woman. Her work keeps her away from home for several days at a stretch.' He grumbles, 'I can't tell her anything. She has overstepped that boundary. At one point, maybe I could have stopped her.' I can almost hear him moan as he says, 'Let her do whatever she wants to do. I am happy for her now.'

I ask him if he knows that his wife was in the famous nude protest in front of the Kangla fort. He says gruffly, 'Yes, I know about the Kangla protest. When they reach that stage, there is no point left in being angry. They took a bold step. I did not know anything about it. I came to know of it much later.'

As I prod him on, he says, 'She's literate, she can write her name. I studied up to class 8. Nobody in my family was directly affected by the conflict. But she was always into social causes – like the local Meira Paibi and Universal Mother Organisation.' He did hear of the Manorama incident. 'I heard about her. My wife was involved in demanding justice for her.'

Then the tensions in the family become apparent. For the past 2-3 years, Ima Sarojini has been staying in the NGO office which is 4-5 km away. 'She comes to meet the grandchildren and daughter. I don't even know if she will be here when I die.'

I am surprised that the old man is still responding to my queries. He tells me, 'I have heard about the AFSPA. I know it's an Act imposed because of militancy, but I am not aware of the details.' His main source of information is the radio from where he gets to know of all the killings in Manipur. 'I don't feel happy about it. I feel equally bad for any life lost – security forces or militants.'

But he is also, in a way, happy that his wife is acting as a watch group. 'She is also engaged in poultry and piggery. She often goes outside Manipur. She goes to Delhi. I don't ask her where and when and she does not bother to tell me either,' he adds. 'My daughters and daughters-in-law take care of me.'

N Bala says that she saw the video of the protest in

the CDs and saw the images in the newspapers. 'I don't know too much about Manorama, but what she (my mother) did was imperative for society,' she tells me.

The absence of Ima Sarojini is however, felt strongly by her family, especially her children. I can sense the disquiet in her house. Bala bites her lip as she tells me, 'I miss all the personal intimacy we had with my mother. I don't get the warmth of my mother's love. If I follow in her footsteps, my child will also be deprived of mother's love.'

As a child, Bala would tremble in fear when military boots marched across the street nearby or when militants hurled a bomb or grenade. I can also sense her desolation as she shuffles around and says, 'When people come and tell me how great my mother is, I wish she could be home more often.'

Afterword

The locality Bamon Kampu Mayai Leikai wears a peaceful look. Just as I gingerly manouvre my way along the narrow lane to Thangjam Manorama's house, I can see photographs that are placed on a table, two of them depicting the state in which her mutilated body was found. They have been placed there for passers-by to pay their tributes.

Manorama's house looks like a usual Meitei household with a courtyard and rooms on all four sides. I can see 63-year-old Thangjam Khumanleima, Manorama's mother, sitting quietly in a corner. Clad in a white phanek, she has hardly spoken since the episode, I learn; her neighbours say that she became quiet soon after her daughter's death, and doesn't even go out. 'I don't want to go out there. It's too painful to see my daughter's photo like that,' she sighs.

Khumanleima often wakes up, startled, in the middle

of the night, screaming 'Mono is coming. Mono is coming'.

Mono – Thangjam Manorama – her favourite child, was picked up by the troops of the Assam Rifles on the night of 10 July 2004. Her bullet-ridden mutilated body was recovered the next morning in an isolated spot not very far from her house in Imphal East, Manipur.

'She often comes in my dreams. She comes with untidy hair. She tells me that she is hungry and asks me to offer food and water. She looks very restless,' says Thangjam Khumanleima, as she squats near her daughter's photograph. Whenever she is visited by this dream, she prepares food and places it in front of the photograph of her 'favourite' child.

After a four-year long agonizing wait for justice, Thangjam Khumanleima took a major decision – to finally perform her daughter's last rites. Manorama's brother Thangjam Dorendra tells me, 'My mother feels she is old and weak. She wants to complete the rituals before she dies. Moreover, till the funeral rites of my sister are over, we cannot perform other religious and social rituals. But our fight for justice will continue.' And so it was that on 11 July 2008 the symbolic funeral pyre was lit by Manorama's elder brother Thangjam Modon and the funeral rites completed.

Dorendra recalls the fateful night when his sister was picked up. 'It was a Saturday and we were watching the film *Raju Chacha* on Doordarshan. At around 12 at night, these security personnel, all men, barged in and asked for her. They questioned her for nearly two hours, showed us an arrest memo and took her away. They told us that she would return the next morning.' In the morning when her dead body was recovered in the woods nearby, the family lodged an FIR and the body was sent for a post mortem. The family refused to accept the body till the guilty were punished. Later the authorities cremated her as an 'unclaimed body'.

Khumanleima, whose name means a 'princess of the Khuman clan', says, 'She was a good daughter. I can't think of anything else. She was a good weaver. She used to think for the good of the community and even taught weaving to young girls.' After her husband Thangjam Birahari's death, it was Manorama, the eldest in the family, who at 14, started shouldering the responsibility of her siblings. 'She used to care for me a lot. I used to act on her advice on any important decision in the family, including guiding my other children. She was very concerned about the future of her siblings. She always kept herself busy and never had a moment of rest. She hardly went out to play with friends,' adds Khumanleima. Manorama was like the 'man' of the house. She told her mother that she would 'get married only when her family's condition is better'.

Khumanleima says, 'She took the upper-hand in arranging her sister's marriages. But she refused to get married herself.' Manorama's sister, Thangjam Inao remembers her sister as 'very strict' who was always confined to her home, weaving clothes. 'I can't forget how she beat up my brother Dorendra as he went out to join in a dance at a community festival. She warned him not to waste time loitering here and there,' she recalls. It is Inao who has inherited Manorama's loom after her death.

'I remember my daughter when I am alone,' says Khumanleima, 'I never thought that she would die such a violent death. If something like this could happen to my daughter, it could happen to anyone.'

Did she ever meet the 12 mothers who staged a nude protest after her daughter's death? 'I did not see the protest,' she says, 'But they came to meet me afterwards. I express my gratitude to those brave women.'

Khumaleima's last wish is to see the AFSPA go. 'This Act has robbed us of our security of life and liberty. Only when it goes will I be sure that my daughter's soul will rest in peace.'

Notes

1. http://www.telegraphindia.com/1060324/asp/northeast/story_6006406.asp
2. https://en.wikipedia.org/wiki/History_of_Manipur
3. http://infochangeindia.org/agenda/claiming-sexual-rights-in-india/written-on-the-body.html
4. Ibohal D.C. and Moirangthem R. 2014. 'Leadership with reference to women police: a study in Manipur', *Journal of Research in Management & Technology*, 11(3): 29–34.